CRUCIAL PROBLEMS IN CHRISTIAN PERSPECTIVE

by Henlee H. Barnette

THE WESTMINSTER PRESS • Philadelphia

Scripture quotations from the Revised Standard Version of the Bible are copyright, 1946 and 1952, by the Division of Christian Education of the National Council of Churches, and are used by permission.

ISBN 0–664–24882–9

LIBRARY OF CONGRESS CATALOG CARD NO.
77–110113

Appreciation is expressed to the following publishers for permission to quote from the works cited: Broadman Press for some of the material in a chapter which I did in *The Gambling Menace,* edited by Rose Coggins, and Alfred A. Knopf, Inc., for "Dream Deferred," copyright 1951 by Langston Hughes, reprinted from *The Panther and the Lash,* by Langston Hughes.

PUBLISHED BY THE WESTMINSTER PRESS ®
PHILADELPHIA, PENNSYLVANIA

PRINTED IN THE UNITED STATES OF AMERICA

Richard B. Douglass

To my mother
Winnie Kerley Barnette
and
to the memory of my father
William Alexander Barnette
(1885–1962)

CONTENTS

PREFACE

OVER THE INTERCOM came the voice of the jet plane's pilot: "This is your captain speaking. Fasten your seat belts, please," he instructed the passengers. "We are entering an area of turbulence."

From a comparatively rural and stable society, Americans in this century have been ushered into numerous areas of political, economic, and social turbulence. The transition from a rather nontechnological era to one of swift transportation, mass communication, exploding knowledge of reality, and space exploration in which astronauts have visited the moon has created a complex matrix for modern man. He finds it difficult to adjust to such a rapidly changing situation.

This is particularly true in the realm of morality. Here man feels himself buffeted about by the fierce gale of moral relativism and plagued with ambiguous ethical standards. Traditional moral norms appear to be inadequate for contemporary decision-making. In our night of moral ambiguities, "all cats appear to be gray."

This volume is written in response to the moral situation in America today. It aims at clarifying the norms of Christian action in relation to some of the crucial problems confronting man in a period of revolutionary change.

Chapter 1 is concerned with moral authority in the decision-making process; Chapters 2, 3, and 4 concentrate on the problem of addiction as expressed in drug abuse, alcoholism, and gambling; moral responsibility in operating an automobile on our streets and highways is dealt with in Chapter 5; Chapter 6 considers the population explosion and methods of control; Chapters 7 and 8 focus on the problems of Black Power and race prejudice; the final chapter takes up the issue of capital punishment.

No book is solely the production of one person. Paul Simmons, instructor in Christian ethics at Southern Baptist Seminary, read the manuscript critically and verified data and sources; Mrs. Robert Shurden and Miss Sue Thrasher typed the rough draft of the manuscript and Miss Jean Aiken did the final draft. Helen, my true helpmeet, provided valuable insights and constant inspiration. To all these persons I am deeply grateful.

H. H. B.

Louisville, Kentucky

1

MORAL AUTHORITY

WHAT IS our moral authority? This is the very heart of our ethical problem today. Many volumes have been written on all aspects of morality; but strangely enough, there are few discussions concerning authority for moral decision and action. Perhaps this fact contributes to the prevalence of so many diverse and contradictory moral theories.

POPULAR MORAL AUTHORITIES

One of the most popular moral theories is summed up in the statement: "Let your conscience be your guide." But the conscience may be badly educated, reflecting only the customs of the community without any transcendent reference.

Some people turn over to a church the task of making moral decisions for them. Here they find the moral authority for their lives. A young man who was "converted" from the Protestant faith frankly admitted that he lived in misery worrying about his sins until he joined the Roman Catholic Church and, as he said: "Let the priest handle the problem of sin and moral decision for me. Now I am quite happy." Of course, the Roman Catholic Church does not teach that one is mechanically forgiven of his sins; but this youth thought so.

But the church itself is a fallible institution. Besides, in the Christian faith, there can be no religion and morality by proxy. Ultimately each one must get his own faith and make his own moral decisions.

Some persons take the Bible as their supreme moral authority, at least in theory. The Bible becomes a "paper pope" to be literally obeyed. Usually exponents of this view pick and choose the ethical passages, often out of context, which they will obey. A lad in grammar school proudly announced to his father that he had practiced the golden rule. He explained that the boy sitting next to him during an examination did not know the answer to a question and this was gladly supplied. "Because," said the lad, "if I had not known the answer, I would have wanted him to give it to me." This, he thought, was "doing unto others as you would have them do unto you"!

Another moral theory gaining popularity in our time is that of emotive ethics. In this theory morality is reduced to feelings. But one cannot trust his feeling in moral matters any more than he can in religion. A pilot of World War II relates how during his training at Kelly Field he was shocked when the instructor told him that he would have to trust implicitly the instrument board on the plane or "it will kill you." The instructor explained that the time would come when the young pilot would feel that he was going in the right direction, but that he must not trust that feeling.

One night it happened. The young pilot relates his experience.

I was alone in a storm in the middle of the night, and I was being tossed around until every strap on my harness was creaking. I had a feeling that my right wing was too low, and so I pulled it up some more. By and by I thought my shoulder straps were too tight. I made up my mind that I was going to loosen them as soon as I got a chance. Then suddenly I came to myself and looked at the instrument board. I was upside down and going in the wrong direction—the words of the instructor came ringing in my ear, "Fly by your instrument board; trust it and not your feelings."[1]

So in the matter of morality, one cannot safely trust one's feelings. Those who do may discover too late that morally speaking they are flying upside down and in the wrong direction!

Common sense, sportsmanship, and foresight alone may also be practical guides in moral decision, but they have no authoritative basis. Furthermore, these moral guidelines are usually seen in subjective terms, and mean different things to different persons. All are too relative to be adequate ethical standards.

TOWARD A CHRISTIAN MORAL AUTHORITY

Any serious search for an authoritative Christian moral standard will involve a reexamination and reformation of one's understanding of the ethical content of the Scriptures.

As has been noted, modern man has largely rejected the Bible as his moral authority and guide. Perhaps this is due to the fact that the Bible has been interpreted too literally by orthodox theologians who tend to find the authority of the Scriptures in theological propositions and prefabricated moral maxims. It must be made plain that Christ is Lord in the Bible and over the Bible. In short, the Bible is a witness to Christ as Lord of the church and the world. Hence, the Lord who governs and guides his children must be sought "beyond the sacred page." Christ is to be found in his full authority as the Word within the words of Scripture. In this sense Jesus Christ becomes the ultimate authority for both character and conduct. An adequate moral authority, therefore, which will be meaningful and relevant for today will be rooted in Christ with love as its motivation and the Holy Spirit as its power.

1. *The Person of the Christian Life.* Christianity is Christocentric, deriving its authority from Jesus Christ as Lord of all existence. Karl Heim rightly observes that the "essence of Christianity does not lie in a philosophy or a system of doctrine, nor in an ethic, but in a Person. Christianity stands or falls with the divine authority of Christ."[2] This Christocentric principle is basic to all ethical action in both personal and social life. Hence, Christ sets us free from rules, yet we are under obligation to make responsible decisions in both small and great matters. Whatever is done is to be done for the glory of God.

Jesous Kurios is the creed of the primitive church and the criterion of the Christian's life (Phil. 2:1–11; Rom. 10:9; 14:9; Eph. 1:20–21). Jesus is Lord of all (Rom. 10:12); all authority is given to him by the Father (Matt. 28:18; John 5:22); he is the cosmic Christ, for all things were made by him and for him. Therefore he must have the preeminence in all things (Col. 1:15 ff.).

Christians of the early church proclaimed Christ as Lord of all life. Christian conduct grows out of the new life in Christ. Paul uses the phrase "in Christ" or some cognate expression, such as "in him" and "in the Lord," more than 160 times to describe the intimate relation between the believer and Christ. To be in Christ is to be a "new creation," a new being (II Cor. 5:17). To be "in Christ" is not only a mystical but a moral union.[3] To be "in Christ" is to have his mind on moral as well as theological matters (Phil. 2:1–11).

The Christian moral imperative, then, is presented not in a code, but in Jesus Christ as Lord. Moral authority, therefore, is not a principle, but a Person. And to believe in Christ is to submit to his Kingship. Hence, he is the ultimate norm of all moral decisions and actions. Paul's charge concerning marriage and divorce is the word of "the Lord" (I Cor. 7:10–11). For Paul "the Lord" always means the living, historical, redeeming One who lived, died, rose again for the saving of men and whose spirit is at work in the church and the world transforming all things. While we do not yet see all in subjection to him, we do "see Jesus" (Heb. 2:8–9).

As Lord of all life, Christ is to be imitated by his followers in their conduct. The Scriptures are replete with the *imitatio Christi* motif. We are to have the "mind of Christ" (Phil. 2:1–11), to love as he loves (John 13:34; Eph. 5:1–2), to be pure as he is pure (I John 3:3), to forgive as he forgives (Col. 3:13), to be long-suffering as he is long-suffering (I Peter 2:21), and to be forbearing as he is forbearing (II Cor. 10:1). In short, the totality of one's being and behavior is to be determined by the character of Christ.

Unfortunately the Kingship of Christ has been largely lost to the theology of the church. His authority for life was substituted by that of the church on the part of some Catholic theologians and the Bible by some Protestants.

Church and Bible became heteronomous forces. The ultimate authority of faith and practice was shifted from Christ to an institution and a book. This transfer of authority to the church is vividly illustrated by a painting in the Cathedral of Cordova in southern Spain. The crucified Christ and the cross upon which he hangs both bend in obeisance before a dark-robed representative of the church. The theological meaning of the painting is that Christ, having completed his work, bowed himself out of history, went into heavenly retirement, and the church took over in his name assuming his authority.

2. *The Principle of Christian Action.* As we have noted, the ultimate norm of Christian action is the Lordship of Christ. Love is the ethical expression of personal faith in him. Paul's ethics is summarized in "faith working through love" (Gal. 5:6). He sees faith, grace, salvation, and good works as being interrelated: "For by grace you have been saved through faith; and this is not your own doing, it is the gift of God—not because of works, lest any man should boast. For we are his workmanship, created in Christ Jesus for good works, which God prepared beforehand, that we should walk in them" (Eph. 2:8–10). Thus "the faith that justifies is not alone—it produces good works through love."[4] What is the nature of love (agape) and how does it relate to good works in personal and social life?

Unfortunately, there is no term in the English language which does justice to the Biblical concept of agape, or love. The word "love" in common parlance is fraught with ambiguity for modern man as seen in the fact that it can mean such things as eroticism, romance, altruism, and affection. There is only one use of the term in the English language where it has a precise and unambiguous meaning—in tennis! In the New Testament, agape is a divine command and appears to mean to will the well-being of others. Agape, therefore, is not merely "liking" someone. Love wills the neighbor's good whether we like him or not. Nor is it simply affection or a feeling for someone, for these cannot be commanded. As C. H. Dodd comments about love, "It is primarily an active determination of the will. That is why it can be commanded, as feelings cannot."[5] Hence, Biblical agape is essentially an action of the will bent on the care of persons.

Agapeic love is neither a legal code nor a detailed road map for life's pilgrimage. Rather it is a "compass" that provides direction, not specific directions, for the conduct of life.[6] In Christian existence, love should become so much a part of life that one does not act in a mechanical manner. The Christian is to enter so completely into the life of God that doing his will may be likened to music. In his book *In Search of England,* H. V. Morton tells of a group that visited the bell tower of Winchester Cathedral, where each visitor was given a bell rope, and then the guide pointed in turn as he wished the individuals to ring the bell. Thus he drew forth from the group the tune "Abide with Me." Commenting on this experience, Donald Baillie states that this was not music, because they did what they were told to do, and that one cannot get music by commandment. Then he contrasts the commanded music of the group with that of a good orchestra engaged in a great symphony. Each member of the orchestra has his own instrument, takes his direction from the conductor, and has so mastered the mechanics that the music sounds creative. Each has the music, is loyal to the conductor, enters into the spirit of the symphony, taking delight in contributing his part with understanding and enthusiasm. The symphony carries them on, lifts them above themselves into a kind of supernatural achievement. The Christian moral life, he concludes, is not a mere matter of "toeing the line," but is a joyous response to the moral demands of God as reflected by the psalmist who declared, "Thy statutes have been my songs in the house of my pilgrimage" (Ps. 119:54).[7]

Agape is all-inclusive. The dimensions of love include neighbor (Matt. 19:19), the brotherhood (I Peter 2:17), and the family (Eph. 5:25). Indeed the range of love includes one's enemies (Matt. 5:44). The Christian is to be all-embracing in his love to others. This is what Jesus meant when he said: "You, therefore, must be perfect, as your heavenly Father is perfect" (Matt. 5:48). In the preceding verses, Jesus declares that we are to love our enemies, for God sends his rain upon the just and the unjust. In other words he is all-inclusive in his love. This is the perfection of which Jesus speaks. The Greek word for "perfect" is *teleiōs,* having to do with the end. A thing is perfect in the Greek sense when it realizes that for which it was made and designed. A fountain pen may be battered and the clip broken; but if it writes, it is a perfect pen because this is the end for which it was made. Man was made in the image of God to be like him in character and deed, and, in this instance, perfection is an all-embracing love for humanity.

Love and justice are inseparable. Agape without justice is sentimental and abstract. Justice socializes love, saving it from being purely personal and sentimental; love humanizes justice, saving it from being rigidly legalistic and unredemptive. Love is the norm of justice, and justice is the instrument of love. In short, justice is love in action in all areas of human existence.

Agape is insight. It is to be accompanied by knowledge and understanding. Our minds get mixed in the syrup of sentimentalism when this fact is ignored. Love, as Paul Ramsey has said, must sometimes "figure the angles."[8] Joseph Fletcher points up this fact in a vivid illustration involving a resident physician on emergency service, deciding whether to give the hospital's last unit of plasma to a young mother of three children or to an old drunk. He concludes that love must make estimates and to prefer the mother *in that situation* is the most loving decision and therefore just.[9]

Paul emphasizes the fact that love and knowledge belong together. He prays for the Philippians that their "love may abound more and more, with knowledge and all discernment, so that you may approve what is excellent," that is, "distinguish between the things that differ" (Phil. 1:9–10). Love must make preferential decisions in concrete situations. "The life of love . . . is not a preference for heart over head, but an encouragement and exercise of every capacity of mind in the service of other people."[10]

Agape is involvement. It is commitment in fulfillment, concern in action. In the incarnation God himself became involved in mankind's sufferings and sorrows because he loved all humanity. To love is to identify with another in his needs, joys, sufferings, and sorrows. To empathetically understand one's neighbor and to serve him at the cost of becoming involved in his troubles is the expression of genuine love. The story of the good Samaritan is a classic example of love in action (Luke 10:29–37). The priest and the Levite, representatives of religion, "passed by" on the other side. The Samaritan, a despised half-breed, "turned aside" to aid the man who had been robbed and beaten. The religion of the Pharisees (Pharisee means "separated one") tended to separate, isolate, and insulate them from human need.

After hearing a lecture on love as involvement, a seminary student told his professor that it was "a terrifying lecture" because he now realized that agape demands involvement in the troubles and sufferings of others. The student frankly stated that he was not sure that he should go on in the ministry because he was fearful of such involvement.

Love in the New Testament sense, then, is distinctive, demanding radical obedience. It was not a matter of mere feeling, but the will bent on achieving the well-being of others. In short, love is spontaneous goodwill toward one's neighbor accompanied by knowledge of *what is* and *ought to be done* in concrete situations under the leadership of the Spirit.

3. *The Power of the Christian Life.* If Christ is the Person, love the ethical principle, then the Holy Spirit is the energizing force of the Christian's existence. He is the enabler of Christian character and conduct. The new birth is the work of the Spirit (John 3:5–8). He guides into all truth (John 16:13–15). The Spirit of God is the Spirit of Christ (Rom. 8:9; Phil. 1:19; II Cor. 13:14). The Christian's relation to God in Christ is not a code but the indwelling Spirit (Gal. 5:5; II Cor. 3:6) who transforms the believer into the "likeness" of Christ (II Cor. 3:18). As Paul declares: "We serve not under the old written code but in the new life of the Spirit." (Rom. 7:6.)

The indwelling of the Spirit is the unique mark of the Christian life (Rom. 8:9). He dwells within both the individual and the church to empower them for moral decision and action (I Cor. 6:19–20; 3:16–17). The fruits of the Spirit are moral, with love as the chief virtue (Gal. 5:22). God's love is poured into the hearts of Christians by the Spirit and is the bond of all Christians (Rom. 5:5; 15:30). Love is the supreme manifestation of the Spirit (I Cor., ch. 13).

Thus life in the Spirit is the life of love. The Christian is to live his whole life in the Spirit. Paul uses three strong verbs to describe life in the Spirit: "walk," "led," and "live" (Gal. 5:16–25). When he says, "Walk by the Spirit" (v. 16), he is referring to conduct. One is to regulate one's life by the Spirit so as not to fulfill the lusts of the flesh. When he urges, "Be led by the Spirit" (v. 18), he is referring to counsel. The Holy Spirit is counselor, leading us into all truth (John 14:26). When Paul admonishes that we "live by the Spirit" (v. 25), he is referring to companionship. The Spirit is called "paraclete" or "one called alongside of" for fellowship. We are to live daily in the companionship of the Spirit. Only as we walk, are led, and live in the Spirit can we live at the high level of love.

In seeking Christian decisions with reference to the moral ambiguities of our day, we measure right action by these criteria: the revelation of God in Christ, radical obedient love tempered with knowledge, and the guidance of the Holy Spirit.

These are the basic elements of an authentic ethic. Love as the central ethical motif is perfectly manifested in Jesus Christ, actualized by the power of the Holy Spirit in the life of the Christian, and oriented toward people in the concrete situation. Simply stated, love means to will the welfare of others so that they may attain "mature manhood" measured by "the stature of the fulness of Christ"

(Eph. 4:13). Any action, ideology, or system that hurts people and hinders them from becoming whole persons stands under the criticism of love.

With these guiding norms of decision and action, we turn to some of the vexing issues confronting people today. Each problem is examined in the light of these standards in terms of their effects upon the achievement of human wholeness.

2

DRUG ADDICTION

THE MASS MEDIA is focusing public attention on the widespread use of hallucinogenic drugs among students at both the high school and college levels as drug abuse in the United States rapidly becomes a national problem. The using of hard drugs such as morphine and heroin appears to be on the increase as indicated in congressional investigations, journals of various kinds, medical and criminal reports, and hundreds of books, both fictional and factual, pouring from the presses. The illegal use of narcotics became a political issue in the 1968 presidential campaign. Voters will recall that Richard Nixon promised to do something about it if elected President.

But Presidents in the past have been baffled as to what to do about drug abuse. For example, President Kennedy requested guidance from the experts at the White House Conference on Narcotics and Drug Abuse held in September of 1962. At that time, he declared: "There is no area in which there is so much mystery, so much misunderstanding, and so many differences of opinion as in the area of narcotics."[1]

If the specialists are not agreed on the nature of drug addiction, what can the layman know about the problem? At best he will simply have to glean what facts he can from reputable writers on the subject, dialogue with drug users, and visits to therapeutic agencies.

DESCRIPTION OF DANGEROUS DRUGS

At least the interested person can become acquainted with the kinds of drugs being used by people today. Dependency-inducing drugs (emotional and/or physical) range all the way from opium to glue. *Narcotic analgesics* (pain-killers) include opium and its derivatives such as morphine, heroin, laudanum, paregoric, codeine, dilaudid, metopon, pantopon. *Synthetic* drugs such as methadone, meperidine, and demerol are substitutes for morphine. Taken regularly these analgesics develop in the user a tolerance (a need for larger doses), physical and emotional dependence, and sickness when withdrawal takes place.

Morphine and heroin, derived from opium poppies, are the drugs most commonly used by the hard-core addicts. The former, first produced in 1817, can be obtained in pills, powders, and capsules. Usually, this drug is injected intravenously with a hypodermic needle. Heroin, discovered in 1898, is a white, powdery material. It may be sniffed through the nose or mixed with cocaine ("snow") or water and taken intravenously. (Most of the addicts use water.) In preparing the dosage, heroin is measured in a spoon. Water is added and the solution is heated by holding a lighted match under the spoon. This makes the ingredients dissolve more quickly and warms the water which provides a "better feeling" when injected into the vein.

When the "cooking" is finished, the liquid is drawn (through a ball of cotton to strain out gums) into a hypodermic, usually an eyedropper with a needle attached. A tourniquet, held by the teeth, is applied to the arm to make the veins more prominent in order to facilitate the injection.

Barbiturates make up a large group of drugs popularly known as "sleeping pills." Among these are phenobarbital-luminal ("purple hearts"), amytal ("blue heavens"), nembutal ("yellow jackets") and seconal ("red devils"). The terms in parentheses are suggested by the colors of the capsules. Many of these are on the market and are used to produce sleep or milder sedation. When taken in large doses barbiturates can produce physical dependence, and withdrawal from them can be more dangerous than from narcotics.[2]

Bromides such as sodium bromide, nervine, and neurosine are prescribed to induce sleep. Though not physically addicting, they may cause emotional dependency. And since there is no physical dependency, no illness results from withdrawal.

Stimulant drugs such as cocaine and amphetamine-type drugs stimulate the central nervous system causing sleeplessness, excitement, and euphoria. Among the amphetamines are benzedrine ("bennies"), dexedrine ("co-pilots"), and diphetamine ("footballs"). Neither cocaine nor amphetamines cause physical dependence and therefore no withdrawal sickness. But they can produce emotional dependence and serious disorders of perception and judgment.[3]

Lysergic acid diethylamide (LSD) is popularly known as a psychedelic (literally, "mind-manifesting") or a mind-stretching drug. It is a synthetic drug composed of d-lyser-

gic acid diethylamide tartrate compounded from a con-
stituent of rye fungus known as ergot. Since it does not
create a physical craving or dependency, there is no withdrawal sickness. However, it may cause emotional dependency.

LSD ("acid") is a powerful drug. A single gram can
provide up to 10,000 doses, each of which may produce
an experience or "trip" up to twelve hours.[4] Though LSD
was discovered in 1938, the public generally knew nothing
of it until Timothy Leary and Richard Alpert, two professors at Harvard, were fired from their posts in 1963 for
involving students in experimenting with the drug.

LSD is a colorless, odorless, tasteless drug and is taken
orally, usually in a sugar cube. The user is "turned on" as
the drug acts to set off a chain of metabolic processes, the
effects of which are felt for several hours. "Travelers" may
have a good or a bad trip, depending on the individual and
dosage. The majority of experiences include a hallucinatory
period in which fantastic visions occur. Some may hear
colors and see sounds. Then comes the "central experience" which constitutes "a good trip." From various
sources, William Braden has constructed a typology of the
core experience. Some of the basic elements are summarized here: (1) the sense of self is lost, but identity is
expanded to include all that is seen and heard, and the
user believes that he has become one with the universe, the
eternal, the absolute; (2) time stops and ceases to be important and the subject is content to exist in the moment;
(3) words lose all meaning and the subject sees objects
as the-thing-in-itself and not the word that symbolizes it;
(4) there are no dualities such as sweet and sour, good and
evil, and the subject is restored to Eden, paradise regained;

and (5) the subject feels he knows all there is to know, namely, ultimate truth. The subject is identical with what he knows and therefore speechless. He is reunited with the Ground of his Being.[5]

A vigorous debate is in process as to the harmful effects of LSD on the user. Adverse reactions in terms of acute pain, extreme fright, and possible toxic effects have been documented by numerous investigators.[6] This drug is not legally available in the United States.

Marihuana is popularly labeled "pot," "tea," "grass," "weed," and "Mary Jane." It comes from the female Indian hemp plant which grows in mild climates the world over. The flowering tops and leaves are chopped into bits and rolled into cigarettes called "reefers," "joints," and "sticks."

There is little data on exactly how the drug works on the human body. More research is needed on this question. As for physical effects the user may become vociferous, unsteady, or drowsy and find coordination of his movements very difficult. There may be a feeling of excitement or depression. Marihuana takes effect about fifteen minutes after the smoke is inhaled. It may cause hallucinations and is therefore classed as a hallucinogen. In the United States it is not legally available since it was outlawed by the Federal Marihuana Tax Act of 1937.

While marihuana is not a narcotic and does not cause physical dependence, it may cause emotional dependence. Moreover, the drug may lead to the use of harder ones like heroin and morphine. It is not true, of course, that every marihuana smoker will become a user of narcotics. But the fact that the social and legal stigma attached to both heroin and marihuana throw the users together, the user of the latter may well take up the use of the former.[7] It stands to reason that a person predisposed to the abuse of one drug may be likely to use stronger ones.

Among other items used as intoxicants to get "high" on are such common things as paint thinners, gasoline, cleaning fluids, and glue. These are inhaled or sniffed through the nostrils. Excessive use of these may prove to be harmful as well as leading to experiments with harder drugs.

PROFILE OF A DRUG DEPENDENT

While an enormous amount of research must be done before we will have any sort of adequate profile of the drug addict, a general picture can be drawn. A drug addict is an individual who has become so physically and emotionally dependent upon a drug that he compulsively uses it to the detriment of self and society. Once "hooked" on a drug, the victim has an overpowering craving for it. Repetitive and increased dosage is necessary to obtain the desired effect. To put it in popular terms, the addict has a "monkey on his back" which must be fed. Discontinuance of the use of narcotic drugs which result in physical dependence causes withdrawal sickness. Other drugs such as bromides, marihuana, cocaine, and benzedrine do not induce physical dependence, and therefore no withdrawal illness, but do cause emotional dependency.

One must avoid drug stereotypes. Drugs differ in chemical composition and in their effects upon persons. Research shows only a few factors as to age, class, and personality traits reflected in addicts. Hence, there is no one personality addiction type. More is known about narcotic addicts than about those who are addicted to amphetamines and other drugs.

Studies show that heroin addiction is most prevalent among men under thirty-five years of age.[8] Of the 60,000 known addicts recorded by the Bureau of Narcotics and Dangerous Drugs, more than half are under thirty years of age. About one out of every four addicts is a female.

A large portion of addicts come from metropolitan centers where addiction is on the increase among minority groups in ghetto areas: Negroes, Puerto Ricans, and Mexican Americans.[9] All indications are that addiction is spreading among the middle and upper classes in suburbia, especially among young people.

Research into the personality of young narcotic addicts reveals a certain pattern of symptoms. Generally, the male addict is described as suffering from a weak ego structure, weak superego functioning, and inadequate masculine identification.[10]

James Mills, an associate editor of *Life* magazine, lived several months with addicts in New York City. He declares that an addict is easily detected by the following factors: (1) he is habitually dirty, his clothes filthy, and he stands slackly as if his body were without muscles; (2) he appears sleepy, moves slowly until he has a fix; (3) he lacks sexual desire; (4) he is childishly immature; (5) he cannot tolerate change; (6) he is morose and restless when he is off heroin; (7) he is extremely narcissistic; and (8) he rejects the notion that he is at fault for his condition.[11]

The addict is constantly preoccupied with the problem of securing enough money to pay for drugs. The cost of maintaining the "habit" mounts from a few dollars to as much as seventy-five dollars per day. It is estimated that in New York City addicts must raise between $500,000 and $700,000 each day, the most of which comes by shoplifting, burglary, forgery, prostitution, and other illegal activities.[12]

The 60,000 known addicts represent only a fraction of those addicted to drugs. Thousands of others hide behind the chemical curtain. The figure does not include those who abuse drugs other than narcotics.

THERAPIES FOR DRUG ADDICTION

A number of governmental and nongovernmental agencies provide treatment for drug addiction. But so far the major attempt to solve the problem in the United States has been that of legal prohibition of the abuse of drugs. The Harrison Act of 1914 has served as a model for most state laws. The act provides that illegal possession and usage of narcotics can mean a fine of $20,000 and a sentence of 5 to 20 years for the first offense, 10 to 40 years for further offenses. A person who sells narcotics to anyone under eighteen forfeits the right to parole and probation for the first offense. If the drug is heroin, he can be sentenced for life in prison or to death. Users of narcotics can draw sentences from 2 to 10 years for the first offense, 5 to 20 years for the second, and 10 to 20 years for further offenses.

Marihuana is regarded as a narcotic by the Government and the penalties for possessing or selling it are almost as severe as those related to heroin. Likewise penalties are stiff for those caught possessing or selling LSD. Conviction can bring a fine of $1,000 to $10,000 and/or imprisonment for up to 5 years. The Bureau of Narcotics and Dangerous Drugs in the Justice Department is the chief agency at the national level active in the enforcement of laws against drug abuse. Narcotics agents operate at the national, state, and local levels.

After nearly forty years of treating the addict as a criminal, a senate committee investigating drug abuse in 1955 concluded that the United States has more addicts than any other country in the world. The Narcotic Addict Rehabilitation Act of 1966 does provide some redeeming features for the addict provided he meets certain tests. An addict who has been charged with a nonviolent federal offense may choose to be committed for treatment instead of being prosecuted. He can be committed to the Surgeon General of the Public Health Service for examination, treatment, and rehabilitation. If he is already convicted of a crime, he may be committed to the Attorney General for a treatment period of not more than ten years. An addict not charged with an offense can be committed for treatment by his own application to the Surgeon General.

The U.S. Government provides two facilities for the treatment of drug addiction. These are the National Institute of Mental Health Clinical Research Center, Lexington, Kentucky, and a similar center at Fort Worth, Texas. At these federal narcotic hospitals, addicts may serve prison sentences for violation of narcotic laws. Volunteer patients are admitted by application.

In these centers the first eight to twenty days are spent in isolation called the withdrawal period. Methadone is substituted for the addict's normal drug because the withdrawal symptoms are milder than those of the opiates. The amount administered is gradually lessened each day. The method of cold turkey, or abrupt withdrawal, is rejected by most medical doctors. Following the withdrawal the patient is given psychological, educational, and vocational evaluations. He may learn basic vocational skills and participate in clubs, athletic and religious activities, along with numerous other programs. The whole program is aimed at preparing the patient for a useful life when he is discharged.

There is a lack of adequate staff in these centers and there is no follow-up program. At the Lexington center, 75 percent of the voluntary patients fail to remain the recommended minimum period of four and one half months. And it is estimated that about 75 percent of the patients who "take the cure" go back to their habit.[13]

Educational institutions have the responsibility of instructing students in the nature of drugs and their effects upon users. Government agencies can attempt, through legislation and law enforcement, to control the drug traffic and reduce the availability of drugs. Among other helping agencies open to addicts are Narcotics Anonymous, Synanon, and Teen Challenge. Organized in 1948, Narcotics Anonymous is structured along the lines of Alcoholics Anonymous. It follows essentially the same program of rehabilitation as does AA. But NA has not been very successful. T. L. Duncan gives the following reasons: (1) discussing drugs in a group may move participants to go out and "get fixed"; (2) pushers sometimes attend the meetings; (3) narcotics squad members infiltrate the group; and (4) addicts are often so dependent that they are unable to provide the necessary strength to maintain a group.[14] Because of these weaknesses and the fact that there are so few NA groups, drug addicts often attend AA groups.

A companion group of the NA is Nar-Anon, which is composed of the wife or husband, parents or children, of the addicts. As in the case of AA's Al-Anon, the purpose of this group is to come together to learn about the nature and problems of addiction and how to be of help to the addict.

The Synanon movement was founded by Charles Dederich in 1958 and has about 1450 addicts living in Synanon centers in four places: Santa Monica, New Haven, San Diego, and Nevada State Prison.[15] Synanon's purpose is to achieve "moral regeneration through the process of education."[16] The program is similar to that of AA, though Dederich discovered that addicts need a firm but understanding authority figure to set limits for them and to keep them within these limits.

All applicants are screened by older members. If accepted, addicts are given the cold turkey treatment (withdrawal without medication); as soon as they are physically able, they are given a work assignment; they participate in group sessions where complete honesty is encouraged. There is a sense of belonging on the part of those living in a Synanon House. It is a way of life for them. But the real force behind the whole movement is Charles Dederich, a strong personality with imagination, understanding, yet firm discipline. In 1969, there were 3500 persons aged seventeen to sixty-one enrolled in the movement.[17]

Teen Challenge is a movement founded by David Wilkerson in 1958. With gifts from churches and individuals, he purchased a house in Brooklyn which became headquarters for a program to help addicts. Attracted by "street services," addicts are brought into the house where services consist of Bible-reading, hymn-singing, and prayer. Wilkerson takes this approach because he believes that it is impossible to cure an addict without God.[18]

As the program began to succeed in reaching and changing some of the youth, a Teen Challenge farm was established in Rehrersburg, Pennsylvania, as a rehabilitation center. In addition, centers have been opened in five other U.S. cities and one in Toronto, Canada.

Before being admitted to Teen Challenge, the addict must present a health certificate showing that he is physically fit. Once admitted, the addict is withdrawn without medication because it is believed that "the sickness of withdrawal will be a deterrent to future use of drugs."[19]

After about a two-week stay at the house in Brooklyn, the addict is taken to the farm. Here a staff of ministers and former addicts conducts classes in Bible, agriculture, woodwork, music, and other subjects. After six to eight months at the farm, those who have been rehabilitated are sent to Bible schools or colleges. Others go back to the city for jobs, and a few remain in the organization as staff members.

A close check is kept on those who have been through the program. Once discharged, the "clean" addict is placed in a church where he will receive encouragement and support. Here he is accepted on the basis that he is now a "new creature" in Christ Jesus. His past life of addiction is considered no problem by the congregation.[20]

THE CHURCH AND DRUG ADDICTION

What is the role of the churches in healing the wounds of an addicted person? Their first task is to become informed about the facts and fictions of drug addiction. Clergymen in particular and laymen in general know little about the problem. Action in relation to this complex issue must be based upon facts. Through educational materials, seminars, and study groups church members can become conversant with the subject of dangerous drugs and drug dependency. A narcotics committee can be established to promote the education of the church about this problem. Basic resources can be secured from agencies such as the American Social Health Association, 1740 Broadway, New York, N.Y. 10019; U.S. Department of Health, Education, and Welfare, Public Health Service, U.S. Government Printing Office, Washington, D.C. 20402; and the Public Information Branch, National Institute of Mental Health, Chevy Chase, Md. 20015.

Several churches in the community could establish a narcotics committee patterned after the East Harlem Protestant Parish Narcotics Committee in New York City. This committee is made up of representatives of seven Protestant denominations and other Protestant groups. The Narcotics Committee offers addicts recreational, psychiatric, medical, and social services as well as spiritual help.

Certainly the churches should undergird and support agencies and persons who work with addicts. Some of the members who have the skills to do so should be encouraged to work with agencies and in projects related to the rehabilitation of addicted persons.

The churches can perform an effective ministry to the families of addicts. Often members of such families suffer a sense of shame, economic distress, and mental frustration. Here the church can bring reassurance, acceptance, and supportive counsel.

Most communities have no agencies to help the "clean" addict to stay that way. Barred from work, ostracized by neighbors, and avoided by former friends, the addict often turns again to his habit. Churches should provide some ministry to these persons. Creative ways of helping them is a moral responsibility. The Neighborhood Council on

Narcotics Addiction located at 306 East 103d Street, New York, N.Y. 10029, will assist in setting up a program to work with addicts.

The pastor of the church is a key person in ministering to the addict. To counsel addicts effectively, the pastor needs to acquire some skills in counseling techniques. Beyond this he must understand that the drug dependent is a physically and an emotionally sick person. He needs someone to listen to him, not to lecture him. The minister must always keep in confidence what he is told by the addict. In the counseling process, he must know when referral is necessary and to whom the referral should be made. An acquaintance with physicians, psychiatrists, and agencies of referral will make the minister's role more effective and easier.

Perhaps most important of all is for the churches to see the whole problem of drug addiction in theological perspective. Unless this is the case, they will not have the courage and the compassion to act redemptively in rescuing the addict.

In theological perspective the addict is a person made in the image of God and this fact makes him worth saving. He is a person "for whom Christ died" and the church must have the courage to care for him. He is the contemporary victim lying on the roadside, beaten, robbed, and waiting for the church to become the good Samaritan. The church must not pass by on the other side.

Drug addicts are "people without a purpose."[21] They lead meaningless lives of loneliness and suffering. Psalm 88, which reflects total despair, is a description of their predicament. The church must provide the gospel of redemption, reconciliation, forgiveness, and salvation. The addict seeks salvation in "a chemical religion." This is his "ultimate concern" and therefore a form of idolatry. Some addicts can be freed from the bonds of addiction only by the power of God.

The addict is a man in agony, in excruciating pain—mental, emotional, and physical. Drugs are pain-killers and a way of temporary relief from suffering. The church must speak relevantly to this human problem. Somehow God's grace must become so powerful in the life of the addict that he can endure the pain of reality without the narcotizing effects of drugs. The love of God must be made so real to him that he will no longer find salvation in chemicals, but in Christ.

The addict is a sick person and must be treated as such. The gospel is a healing power. The threefold ministry of Christ was teaching, preaching, and healing. The church would do well to lay more stress on the healing ministry in relation to people whose lives are broken physically and spiritually. Is there no balm in Gilead for the social lepers of this age?

The person hooked on psychoactive drugs is a lonely person. He feels alienated from God and God's people and therefore seeks fellowship in a "pill party." But he eventually discovers that he is without authentic interpersonal relations. The church should provide a koinonia, a fellowship of sharing, where the clean as well as the unclean addict can break through the chemical walls that separate them from God's people and find relationships that make for mutual understanding, hope, and affection.

The addict has a problem of guilt. Most addicts know that they are doing something illegal when they start taking narcotics. Therefore, they have a sense of guilt that they may not even admit to themselves. They bear a sense of shame for the crimes they have committed to themselves and to society. Ultimately this kind of guilt can be resolved in some addicts only by the power of God.[22] The task of the church is to help the addict to see that God really forgives sin. In turn the addict must be convinced that God accepts him and that he can accept God's acceptance of the unacceptable.

Drug addiction is a complex problem. There are no easy solutions. To get at the facts, more research is imperative. The church has a responsibility in this effort to free those who are enslaved to the power of drugs. Its mission is that of Christ's: "To proclaim release to the captives and recovering of sight to the blind, to set at liberty those who are oppressed." (Luke 4:18.)

3

ALCOHOLISM

DRUNKENNESS IS AT LEAST as old as Noah, who planted a vineyard, overindulged in the fruit of the vine, and shamed his sons (Gen. 9:20–22). From that day to this, the toll that alcohol has taken in terms of premature death, crime, broken bodies, homes, and communities makes a sad and sordid story.

At present, alcoholism has become the fourth major health problem in the United States, exceeded only by heart disease, cancer, and mental illness. Over five million persons in the United States are alcoholics. This means that there is hardly a home that is not touched by this problem. Those who carry the alcoholic cross do not bear it alone.

Yet there is a strange silence about alcohol and alcoholism among clergymen and theological professors. Ministers rarely ever approach the subject. Perhaps they feel that Protestantism took too much of a beating for being the prime supporter of national prohibition. It may be an off-limits subject for the academician because of the fear of being moralistic and prohibitionist. Hence, the problem is left to the medical doctor, the scientists, and the social worker.

It is true that moralistic approaches to the ingestion of alcohol can worsen the issue, but this is no justification for the preacher and the professor to sweep it under the rug or to pretend that it lies beyond the scope of their responsibility. Rather, the hurt and the destruction stemming from the misuse of alcohol should serve as a stimulus for the church and the seminary to discover creative and redemptive ways of coping with it.

SOME MYTHS OF ALCOHOL

Back in the hills of North Carolina when I was a boy I used to hear the story of the hoop snake. According to the story, the hoop snake could take its tail between its fangs, make a hoop of itself, and roll after a man with deadly precision. This particular species had a needlepoint filled with poison on the end of its tail which struck the victim as the snake released his hold. If the snake missed a man and struck a tree, according to the tradition, the tree would die before sundown.

Now, some of the people around that part of the country actually believed this story. To this day hoop snakes roll through our lives, statements of alleged truth that could never be true, but appear to be true because some people believe them.

There is a multitude of hoop-snake myths about drinking alcoholic beverages. The explosion of some of these will help to clear the underbrush on the way to some facts about alcohol.

A popular myth is that some people are born alcoholics. Most specialists agree that, while it is probable that persons can inherit the inability to control alcohol due to constitutional structure, there is nothing in heredity that compels them to use it. "Psychologically," says Robert Seliger, M.D., "imitation and identification give many individuals a feeling of this pseudoinheritance."[1] The heredity fallacy is one alibi for consuming alcoholic beverages.

Becoming drunk is often referred to as getting "tight," but actually the result is "looseness." Under the influence of drink, the individual develops a loose tongue which sometimes gets him into a tight place. He utters words that later he regrets. His inhibitions are loosened, and he may find himself engaged in premarital or extramarital sexual relations that can prove to be embarrassing and harmful to himself and to his family.

The relaxation myth is another one to be exploded. Used as an escape hatch from worry, anxiety, and boredom, alcohol may provide temporary relief. It may anesthetize the pain and provide momentary "peace of mind," but the potential danger and consequent damage to the individual may outweigh the pleasure derived.

There is another superstition that deserves to be debunked and that is the notion that alcohol warms up the body in cold weather. The fact is that only the skin warms up while internal heat is lost. This happens because alcohol dilates the blood vessels on the surface of the human body. Consequently, the greater flow of blood to the surface dissipates the heat in the body.

Then there is the myth that anyone can learn to drink in "moderation." There is a gamble here. Moderate or "social" drinking may be the first step to overindulgence. It is impossible to tell whether or not moderation may lead to chronic alcoholism. This fact was impressed upon the writer by a superintendent of a large hospital for alcoholics.

He declared that almost without exception the inhabitants of the hospital began their path to alcoholism as social drinkers (moderate drinking can lead to immoderate drinking). The surest way to avoid excessive drinking is to refuse the first drink.

Then there is the myth that an alcoholic can learn to drink in moderation. The argument that he can control his drinking is sheer nonsense. The chronic drinker can be "cured" for years and, with one drink, be back on the bottle.

Some are deceived into thinking that drinking makes one "come alive" with sharpened senses. But it is a known fact that alcohol is, pharmacologically, a drug that acts as a depressant and not a stimulant. E. M. Jellinek, well-known authority on alcohol, notes that one ounce slows the reaction time to a visual stimulus by approximately 6 percent.[2] This may slow down reflex coordination just enough to cause a driver to miscalculate the changing of the stop light or the distance of another car.

Some drink to assert their individuality, to "be a man." Actually, alcohol destroys one's individuality. The alcoholic becomes dependent on alcoholic beverages to escape from reality. There is a regression to a childlike state of dependence upon the bottle, family, and friends. The alcoholic becomes more and more dependent upon outside forces for support to the neglect of the resources within himself.

The above are only a few of the myths that are associated with alcohol. But myths make it difficult to get at the *facts* about the problem. Just who is an alcoholic? Is there a distinct alcoholic personality? With the help of the students of alcoholism, we turn to deal with these questions.

Who Is an Alcoholic?

The World Health Organization (WHO) describes alcoholics as "those excessive drinkers whose dependence upon alcohol has attained such a degree that it results in noticeable mental disturbance, or in an interference with their bodily and mental health, their interpersonal relations, their smooth social and economic functioning or those who show the prodromal signs of such developments."[3] Howard J. Clinebell, Jr., provides the following definition of what he means by the term "alcoholic": "An alcoholic is anyone whose drinking interferes frequently or continuously with any of his important life adjustments and interpersonal relationships."[4] E. M. Jellinek defines alcoholism as *"any use of alcoholic beverages that causes any damage to the individual or society or both."*[5] These two latter definitions are more vague, but they provide operational definitions that encompass various kinds of alcoholics and alcoholism.

Is there an alcoholic personality? Efforts to identify specific traits in the personality of the alcoholic have not met with success. There appears to be no specific type of personality related to alcoholism. While alcoholics in general come from a poor "psychologic environment," no particular neurosis can be designated which is typical of alcoholics.[6]

However, it is possible that there are certain character or personality traits that tend to appear in certain persons, plus membership in *"highly prone social groups,* [which] *make for a predisposition or a vulnerability to alcoholism."*[7] While there is no single alcoholic personality, psychiatrists detect characteristics that frequently appear, either alone or in combination. Neil Kessel and Henry

Walton designate these as the immature, self-indulgent, self-punitive, "stressed" personalities, often with sex problems.[8]

Compulsive drinkers want to be popular, well-liked, and loved. Sociable and vociferous, they seem compelled to seek approval of others. This inordinate wish to be loved points to "a great underlying feeling of insecurity, a feeling which must constantly be denied, compensated for, or anesthetized."[9]

SOME CAUSES OF ALCOHOLISM

Few facts are known about the causes of alcoholism. It is generally agreed that alcohol itself is not the cause, but only the vehicle of this condition. "Alcoholics are made," says Lawrence Wooley, M.D., "not by alcohol, but by people who use it."[10] Clinebell puts it: *"Alcoholism comes in people, not in bottles."*[11] If this is true, then we must look within to find elements resident in the person that make for this condition and in the evironment for factors that evoke its manifestation.

Obviously there is no one cause within or without the person which makes him an alcoholic. Hence, there must be a "multiple etiology," a constellation of causes. Theories of causation, therefore, fall under three main categories: physiological, psychological, and sociocultural.

Among the physiological causes of alcoholism, the specialists suggest inherited peculiarities of the organism; a nutritional deficiency brought on by an inherited metabolic abnormality such as an endocrine imbalance, a genetically inherited emotional makeup of a person responsible for the craving for alcohol, and certain chemical elements in the blood which bring on alcoholism.

All these "causes" are still theories. None have been proven to be *the* cause of alcoholism. Hence, the search goes on for some hidden factor in chronic alcoholism, yet to be discovered.

Psychological theories generally focus on personality characteristics. Alcoholism is seen as a symptom of a disturbance in the character structure of personality. Ruth Fox declares that "alcohol addiction may be a symptom of any underlying personality maladjustment; that the soil in which alcoholism grows is almost always the neurotic character; that this neurotic pattern was formed in infancy or early childhood because of disturbances in the relationship of the child to the significant persons with whom he came in contact."[12] Thus the psychological dimension of alcoholism only points up the complexity of the problem.

Among the personality traits that show up in the alcoholic in various combinations are these listed by Ronald J. Catanzaro: high level of anxiety, emotional immaturity, ambivalence toward authority, low frustration tolerance, grandiosity, low self-esteem, feeling of isolation, perfectionism, guilt, compulsiveness, anger over dependency, sex role confusion, and inability to express angry feelings adequately.[13]

Perhaps we should add to the above list of traits the fact that the alcoholic feels compelled to make himself popular and is sometimes skilled at this. He will deprive his family of necessities by buying drinks for others in order to gain approval. Another trait that he exhibits is that of talkativeness. He seems to get some oral satisfaction from being vociferous.

As in the case of physiological causation theories of alcoholism, psychological ones are not conclusive. The above personality traits appear in people who do not become alcoholics. Why do not all neurotic persons become chronic alcoholics? Must we not admit that there is no one personality type of alcoholic and that we are not sure as to just what combination of traits make for alcoholism? More research will have to be done before these questions can be firmly answered.

Research into the sociocultural causes of alcohol is still in its infancy. Studies appear to show that an inadequate family background may produce alcoholics. Paternal factors in terms of authoritarianism, success worship, moralism, and overt rejection, it is thought, produce the "soil of addiction."[14] Some stress the view that family conflict, the alcoholic behavior of parents, parental punitiveness, and a lack of supervision of the child are related to the development of alcoholics.[15]

Neil Kessel and Henry Walton conclude that the most effective way to foster excessive drinking is by example and that the family is the chief agent.[16] They reason that if the parents drink in moderation, the child is unlikely to become an alcoholic. If parents are rigid teetotalers, the child may become fanatical in his own attitude toward drink. Should he need to express rebellion against his parents, he may become as fervently alcoholic as they are abstinent.[17]

Social pressure plays a significant role in drinking. At social gatherings and parties where alcoholic beverages are served, some persons feel out of place if they do not drink. They feel that they must take a drink "to be sociable." Peer influence on adolescent drinking has been found to be strong. Pressure to drink is widespread at parties attended by high school students and in high school clubs.

Availability of alcohol is directly related to the incidence of alcoholism. It is an occupational hazard for those employed in the liquor business, salesmen, officers in the military, and young executives. The last three groups frequently meet at bars for fellowship and to transact business.

It must also be noted that the number of drinking places in a community is a factor in the amount of alcohol consumed. One is more likely to visit a liquor store or tavern nearby than one across town. Where alcoholic beverages are readily available, more people will drink and drink more frequently.

Suggestions through the mass media is a powerful force in shaping human behavior, including drinking habits. In almost every movie and TV program drinking is depicted. Here the liquor industry receives millions of dollars' worth of free advertising for their product. In addition, liquor manufacturers spend millions of dollars on advertising in the slick magazines. *Playboy* magazine alone receives over one-half million dollars for each issue for advertising alcoholic beverages. The newspapers and billboards also carry liquor ads. Attractive and expensive colored booklet inserts in the daily newspapers with instruction on "how to make 46 great drinks at home" frequently appear. The idea is to get liquor *in the home* for the family to enjoy it.

Liquor and beer ads are presented as a part of "happy living" and as being normal and customary. Consumers are portrayed as living in beautiful and well-furnished homes. Alcoholic beverages are associated with patriotism, sports, recreation, success, and all-round happy and healthful living. Always it is identified with the beautiful, the wholesome, the virile, and the good. The implication is obvious: life with liquor is the *summum bonum*. The producers of alcohol never dare to show the results produced in terms of millions of broken lives, homes, communities, nor do they even hint at the 25,000 deaths annually on our highways associated with drunken driving.

It is an interesting fact that almost no writer on the subject of alcohol and the destructiveness which results from its use lays any responsibility on the manufacturers of this product. They get off scot-free from any blame for its widespread destruction of the life, health, and happiness of millions.

One wonders why the Surgeon General of the United States, who pointed out the harmful effects of cigarettes so that now a warning must be printed on every package, has not made a study of the effects of alcohol on the health of those who use it. At present there are serious efforts to ban all cigarette advertising. Why should not a warning be printed on bottles and cans of alcoholic beverages as to its harmful effects? Alcohol is health problem number four in the nation. The number of alcoholics increases at a frightening rate. Why should this nation permit the advertising of alcoholic beverages, the ravages of which are much greater than that of cigarette smoking?

Plato, the philosopher, declares that "the habit of drinking is not to be encouraged by the state."[18] By its neglect to curb the liquor traffic by adequate legislation and enforcement, the Government is indirectly encouraging citizens to drink. Indeed, more alcoholic beverages are consumed in our capital city of Washington than in any other city of comparable size in the nation.

UNDERSTANDING AND UNDERGIRDING THE ALCOHOLIC

The church and the community have the resources and the responsibility to help the alcoholic and his family. Both religious and social therapies are essential in healing the chronic drinker. Team action is necessary if the alcoholic is to receive the optimal treatment for his rehabilitation. This cooperative action must be based upon an understanding of the alcoholic and the nature of his affliction.

1. *The Church and the Alcoholic.* Churches in America differ in their attitudes toward drinking alcoholic beverages. Roman Catholic, Anglican, and Lutheran churches tend to accept the principle of moderation in drinking, though each has voluntary abstinence groups. Methodists, Baptists, and other Protestants generally take the abstinence stance. But all church groups recognize alcoholism as a serious problem. Certainly all churches should take a redemptive approach to the alcoholic's plight.

a. *Alcoholism: sin or sickness?* Some church leaders have tended to take the attitude that alcoholism is primarily a sin. Alcoholics behave as they do because of moral depravity. Hence, the problem is labeled as a vice.[19] Dr. Howard J. Clinebell, Jr., made a study of the attitude of clergymen who attended the first seven years of the Yale Summer School of Alcohol Studies and found that the 146 who responded to a survey believed that alcoholism begins in sin and ends in sickness.[20]

Specialists are generally agreed that alcoholism is a disease.[21] If not a disease by itself, it may be a symptom of illness, "a symptom of deep or deeper underlying personality emotional reactions of varying degrees and types."[22] Dr. Carroll Wise declares: "The Alcoholic is not sick because he drinks but . . . drinks because he is sick, and then becomes doubly sick."[23]

Some fear that to label alcoholism as a disease is to

imply that the alcoholic is not responsible for his condition and conduct. But the vast majority of those who speak of alcoholism as a sickness do not say that the alcoholic is not morally responsible for his behavior. Treatment always involves responsible action on the part of the chronic drinker.

Father John C. Ford, S.J., who believes that alcoholism is both sin and sickness, has indicated the moral element in this sickness. With regard to the moral problem there is the question of the sin of deliberate intoxication, of one's responsibility for sinful acts while drinking, of the responsibility of an alcoholic for becoming an alcoholic, of the responsibility of the alcoholic for his excessive drinking after he has become an alcoholic, and the question of the alcoholic's responsibility for doing something about his drinking after he has discovered that he is an alcoholic.[24] Father Ford believes that alcoholism is a "triple sickness of body, mind, and soul." When talking to clergymen, he stresses the idea of the sickness of the alcoholic; and in speaking to psychiatrists or sociologists, he insists on the idea that there are moral problems involved.[25]

No doubt the debate will continue as to whether alcoholism is sin or sickness. The main thing for the church is to have the courage to care for the alcoholic.

b. *Biblical perspective on alcohol and its use.* The attitude of the church toward alcohol and alcoholics should be determined by the Bible. It cannot be denied that the Bible recognizes as acceptable a moderate use of wine as a beverage (I Tim. 5:23). Wine was used by our Lord when he instituted the "Last Supper," and at the wedding feast at Cana he turned water into wine for the guests (John 2:1 ff.). Jesus himself was accused by his enemies as being "a gluttonous man, and a winebibber" (Luke 7:34). The point is that nowhere does the New Testament condemn the moderate use of wine.

Any attempt to find a distinction between two kinds of wine in the New Testament, the one intoxicating and the other unintoxicating, is futile.[26] In the one instance where the Greek equivalent (*gleukos*) of the Hebrew *Tirosh* (commonly translated "new wine") is used the context clearly indicates that it is intoxicating (Acts 2:13).

But there are strong warnings against the misuse of wine in both the Old and the New Testaments. Drunkenness is condemned in unambiguous terms (Isa. 5:11; Matt. 24:49; Luke 12:45–46; I Cor. 6:10; 11:21; Rom. 13:13; Eph. 5:18; I Tim. 3:3; I Peter 4:3). The author of Proverbs clearly describes the consequences of strong drink: "Who has woe? Who has sorrow? Who has strife? Who has complaining? Who has wounds without cause? Who has redness of eyes? Those who tarry long over wine, those who go to try mixed wine." (Prov. 23:29–30.)

While total abstinence is not taught in the Scriptures, a good case can be made for it. Two groups of total abstainers are mentioned in the Old Testament: the Nazirites and the Rechabites (Num. 6:3–4; Jer. 35:1–11). In the New Testament there are positive guiding principles of abstinence. Church historian Ronald Bainton cites the following: (1) care of the body as the temple of God (I Cor. 6:15, 19) and (2) concern for the weaker brother (Rom. 14:21).[27] These are basic principles, not laws, and should be followed for one's own sake and for the sake of those who may become alcoholics.

In relation to those who are victims of alcohol, the church must act redemptively if it is to do the will of God. It is the purpose of God to redeem all men regardless of their condition. To identify with God's purpose is "to bind up the brokenhearted, to proclaim liberty to the captives, and the opening of the prison to those who are bound" (Isa. 61:1).

There are concrete ways in which the church can help redeem and rehabilitate the alcoholic. The church may not know much about alcoholism, but it possesses the gospel which transforms human life. The proclamation of the good news aims at the conversion of the individual. The psychologist calls this experience the "re-centering of personality." The psychiatrist defines conversion of the alcoholic as a "psychological event in which there is a major shift in personality manifestation."[28] Francis W. McPeek concludes that such commitment to the living God has "accounted for more recoveries from the disease [alcoholism] than all the other therapeutic agencies put together."[29]

McPeek's statement may appear to be extravagant, but psychiatrists do recognize conversion as a therapeutic approach to alcoholism. While Karl Menninger holds that psychoanalysis is the only treatment technique for the complete and thoroughgoing reconstruction of personality, he admits that he knows of instances where it occurs as a "result of religious conversion."[30]

A religious conversion may be the only hope for some alcoholics. In the 1930's an alcoholic who was director of a large chemical company in America went to see Carl Jung, the famous Swiss psychiatrist, for help. Jung informed him that his only hope of salvation was "a spiritual experience."[31] Later this man became one of the prefounders of Alcoholics Anonymous.

Conversion in the Christian sense involves a turning away from an egocentric orientation to the centering of personality in Christ. This requires a sense of helplessness to redeem one's own self and surrender to a power greater than self. The act of complete surrender is essential in the case of the alcoholic.[32] This is the religious element of the AA movement. The alcoholic must recognize God's help in his struggle. The apostle Paul puts it: "I am nothing— I can do all things through Christ" (Phil. 4:13).

c. *Koinonia: therapeutic community.* One of the basic needs of the alcoholic is fellowship in small groups. It would be cruel to get an alcoholic "converted" and expect him to find the support he needs in a large, impersonal congregation. He must find a fellowship of radical sharing in an intimate group. Within the ecclesia there must be formed small groups of people who care and who will undergird both the alcoholic and his family. The alcoholic must feel free to call any member of the koinonia and at any hour of the day or night for help.

The early "church in thy house" pattern in which small groups of Christians gathered for spontaneous prayer, Bible-reading, singing, and testimony, food and drink, should be recovered. In this atmosphere the converted alcoholic could find the spiritual counterpart of the tavern. Here he could feel accepted and understood among his fellow believers.

d. *Pastoral counseling.* Alcoholics need pastoral care and counseling. Clergymen should not be content to direct routinely the chronic drinker to the psychiatrists and to treatment centers. Clinebell thinks that the eventual goal in counseling the alcoholic is to relate him "to those therapeutic groups or agencies which are specifically designed to help him with his problem."[33] If he means that the pastor's role is to confer casually with the alcoholic and then shift him over to the specialists, he ignores the significant contribution the clergyman can make to the chronic drinker.[34]

To refer the alcoholic too quickly may leave him with the feeling that he is being rejected by the clergyman. If the minister establishes rapport with the alcoholic, referral may be easier and more successful. He will be better prepared emotionally for the aid which the specialist can provide. Hence, the minister should take time to counsel with the alcoholic long enough to awaken confidence and trust before referral. Even after referral the pastor's task is not ended. He should keep in touch with his counselee and assure him that the door is open for further dialogue.

Obviously the desperately ill alcoholic should be immediately referred to those persons and agencies which can provide medical and psychiatric help. It is all-important for the pastor to understand the various stages of alcoholism. Inability to know when referral is necessary may prove to be disastrous for the alcoholic.

Preparation for counseling the alcoholic is imperative. Clinebell suggests several prerequisites: (1) a basic understanding of alcoholism; (2) training in the general principles and techniques of counseling; (3) insights into the literature concerned specifically with counseling alcoholics; (4) if possible, attendance at an institute or school on alcohol; (5) acquaintance with the resources available for referral in the community.[35]

Above all, the pastor must have genuine concern for the care of the alcoholic as a person. His knowledge of the techniques and the intricate theories of counseling may not be on a par with the specialists. But if the pastor has a deep love for the loveless victim of drink, he can play a significant role in his redemption and rehabilitation.

Obviously the minister will be hard put to counsel adequately with the alcoholics and their families in his community. Hence, he should follow the pattern of the primitive church and equip the laity to share in this task. After all, the equipment of the saints for the work of the ministry is one of his basic responsibilities (Eph. 4:10–12). Indeed the whole congregation is to serve as counselors in one way or another (Gal. 6:1 f.). This is the meaning of the priesthood of all believers. Some members could be trained to deal specifically with alcoholics. Often a layman may be more effective in motivating the alcoholic to seek help than all the pastors in the ministerial association.

2. *The Community and the Alcoholic.* Fortunately the church is not alone in its ministry to the alcoholic. There are resources for his rehabilitation in the community. Teamwork including the church, the medical doctor, the psychiatrist, and the special agencies equipped to deal with the alcoholic's problem is indispensable.

a. *Community resources.* Some communities have a greater number of resources for the rehabilitation of problem drinkers than others. But generally the following exist in communities across the nation: the physician, the psychiatrist, the nurse, the social case worker, and the trained helping person (a part-time, trained person on a team of workers). Agencies include hospitals, rescue missions, the local committee on alcoholism (affiliated with the National Committee on Alcoholism), rest farms, halfway houses, outpatient clinics, foster homes, community houses, social centers, and Alcoholics Anonymous.

b. *Alcoholics Anonymous (AA).* AA is considered to be the most effective organization at present in redeeming the alcoholic and therefore deserves special attention. Perhaps AA brings more alcoholics to a sober life than all other agencies combined.[36] Why is this group so successful in rehabilitating the alcoholic? How does it work?

AA is a fellowship of men and women who share their experience, strength, and hope with one another in order to solve their common problem of alcoholism and to help others to do the same. Basic to the group is the Twelve-Step Program for a New Way of Life:

Twelve Steps of Alcoholics Anonymous

1. We admitted we were powerless over alcohol—that our lives had become unmanageable.
2. Came to believe that a Power greater than ourselves could restore us to sanity.
3. Made a decision to turn our will and our lives over to the care of God *as we understood Him.*
4. Made a searching and fearless moral inventory of ourselves.
5. Admitted to God, to ourselves, and to another human being the exact nature of our wrongs.
6. Were entirely ready to have God remove all these defects of character.
7. Humbly asked Him to remove our shortcomings.
8. Made a list of all persons we had harmed, and became willing to make amends to them all.
9. Made direct amends to such people wherever possible, except when to do so would injure them or others.
10. Continued to take personal inventory and when we were wrong promptly admitted it.
11. Sought through prayer and meditation to improve our conscious contact with God *as we understood Him,* praying only for knowledge of His will for us and for the power to carry that out.
12. Having had a spiritual awakening as a result of these steps, we tried to carry this message to alcoholics, and to practice these principles in all our affairs.[37]

In this series of steps are the elements of a "conversion" experience: recognition of powerlessness, commitment to

God, honesty with self, confession of sin, prayer for forgiveness, restitution, continued self-analysis, confession, prayer for a knowledge of God's will and power to do it, and witness to others.

Slogans appear throughout the literature of AA and on posters at meetings which express key ideas and encouragement. Among these are: "Live and let live" (tolerance), "Keep an open mind" (new ideas), "Easy does it" (relaxation), and "But for the grace of God" (thankfulness and dependency upon God). The "serenity prayer" is also a source of strength for the alcoholic. It reads: "God grant me the serenity to accept the things I cannot change, courage to change the things I can, and wisdom to know the difference."[38]

Alcoholics Anonymous has allies in Al-Anon and Alateen. The former is a fellowship of nonalcoholic husbands, wives, relatives, and intimate friends of alcoholics. The latter seeks to help the children of alcoholics to understand the nature of alcoholism and in this way make it easier for them to adjust emotionally to their parent's problem. In their meetings, members of Alateen seek to understand, share, and solve their common problems.[39]

We have stressed that church and community must work as a team for the redemption and rehabilitation of alcoholics. Basic to dealing with these sick people are humility, understanding, and controlled empathy. One should never moralize in dealing with the chronic drinker. "But by the grace of God I am what I am." (I Cor. 15:10.) This is the affirmation of the ancient apostle and the modern AA member. It should be every man's, for it is only by the grace of God that he is not an alcoholic or something worse.

4

GAMBLING

GAMBLING IS AN ACT of betting by two parties whereby property is transferred from one to the other on the basis of chance. As a result of the event one pays and the other receives. It is estimated that more than fifty million Americans engage in some form of gambling and that about six million are compulsive addicts. These compulsives have the gambling fever that keeps going up, cannot be cured, but can be arrested. Few recognize that compulsive gambling is as extensive as alcoholism and, like the latter, may result in the destruction of personality, as well as the family, and often leads to a life of crime.

A spate of literature has been published concerning the nature, the extent, the evil effects, and the control of gambling. Almost nothing has been written on the rehabilitation of the gambler from the medical and psychiatric point of view. Apparently no material by the church exists on this issue. To my knowledge there is not a single article in pastoral care or pastoral psychology journals on counseling the compulsive gambler or even the moderate one. It is difficult to find any material in depth in any religious literature which is specifically related to this problem. When I informed Dr. Wayne Oates, professor of psychology of religion at the Southern Baptist Theological Seminary, Louisville, Kentucky, that writing on this subject was like making "brick without straw," he replied, "Yes, and you will have to make your bricks without Oates because I am not aware of any material on the subject."

At present, resources for helping the gambler are scanty. The remaining part of this discussion is aimed at describing these few resources and offering suggestions for developing others. As outlined, these resources are not necessarily in order of importance.

COMMUNITY RESOURCES

An arbitrary distinction is made between community and church resources in order to emphasize the role of the latter in the care of the gambler.

1. *Psychiatric Aid.* Among community resources that are available to gambling addicts is that of psychiatric help. As in the case of the alcoholic, the compulsive gambler is a sick person. An eminent doctor holds that alcoholism, gambling, and superstition is a triad that has essentially the same causal factors. On the basis of clinical experience, he discovered that these patients carried into adulthood emotional and psychological dynamics that belong to the preadolescent and childhood periods.[1]

So deep-seated are the psychodynamics of gambling that the psychiatrists are still searching for the roots of the problem. Sigmund Freud relates pathological compulsion for gambling to the conflict over masturbation. The addiction for gambling becomes an unconscious substitute for masturbation and affords self-punishment for it.[2] Dr. Ralph

R. Greenson relates gambling to satisfaction for latent homosexual, oralreceptive drives, and gratification of unconscious needs for punishment.[3]

The truth of the matter is that neither the psychiatrist nor the gambler knows definitely the causative forces in compulsive gambling. Recently I called a psychiatrist for clinical information regarding this problem. It so happened he had no more information that I had; he was at that moment reading Gamblers Anonymous literature in preparation for helping a patient. Nevertheless, the psychiatrist can be of help to severe pathological cases. Also he can refer the compulsive gambler to Gamblers Anonymous.

2. *Gambling Education.* An educational approach to the problem of gambling may be made through high schools and colleges. In some states lectures are given in secondary schools on the nature of alcohol and danger in its use. Since the problem of gambling is almost as great as that of alcoholism, some discussion of this issue should take place at the secondary school level. Colleges and universities could have lectures and courses bearing on the subject. We have a moral obligation to inform students of the debilitating effects of gambling upon the gambler, the family, and society at large.

The old argument that education cannot help to eradicate the "natural instinct" to gamble does not hold. Cannibalism is a natural instinct of primitive people. Civilized people do not eat other human beings, as did our English forebears in A.D. 4. Through proper education man can be trained to channel his natural impulses into constructive action. His natural instincts can be redirected through the educational process to wholesome expressions.

3. *School of Gambling Studies.* An enormous amount of research needs to be done before much can be accomplished toward redeeming the gambling addict. Therefore, schools and institutes on gambling should be established similar to the Yale Center of Alcohol Studies. Team research study which would encompass all aspects of the problem and dissemination of such information would aid in coping with the gambling racket and the gambling personality.

4. *Counseling Center.* A counseling center could be established in the community to aid the gambler and his family. Of course, it should be staffed with competent persons. Some professional people may volunteer their time and services for this project. Referrals could be made to mental health clinics, psychiatrists, social welfare services, Gamblers Anonymous, and Gam-Anon, wives' groups.

5. *Study Committee on Gambling.* Every community can organize a committee to study the local problem of gambling. Action on such a complex issue must be undergirded with facts. Too many moral crusades have gone on blindly without adequate legal and sociological data. The results have usually been negative so far as curbing and controlling gambling is concerned.

The strategy of the committee should be to do its work without fanfare and without eyes on the camera and news headlines. Able people should be engaged to do the research. Once the facts are in hand, concerned citizens should arouse the public conscience and engage in practical action to rid the community of the gambling forces. An example of such action occurred in Newport, Kentucky, by a well-informed and well-organized Citizens Committee a few years ago.

6. *Preventive and Protective Laws.* Citizens can participate in action to provide legislation for the reduction of facilities and inducements to gambling. Where there are available means of gambling, even the "recovered" gambler will be strongly tempted to gamble. As far as possible the community should protect all its citizens from the temptations to evil.

Moreover, concerned citizens can insist upon strict enforcement of existing laws on gambling. Every citizen can register his opposition to the passage of legislation to make gambling legal by writing to his representatives in government. Letters to governors, state senators, and congressmen often determine which legislation will become law.

Unless good men act, evil forces will take over a community. Gambling is often tied to crime syndicates which capture communities and operate like a tapeworm in the intestines. Such parasitic forces make communities weak, sickly, and terror-ridden.

7. *Gamblers Anonymous.* One of the sources to which the compulsive gambler can go for help is Gamblers Anonymous, an organization patterned after Alcoholics Anonymous. Organized in 1957 at Los Angeles, California, it is a fellowship of men and women who share their experience, strength, and hope with one another that they may solve the common problem and help others in the same plight.

Compulsive gambling is described by GA as "an illness, progressive in nature, which can never be cured, but can be arrested."[4] The only requirement for membership is the desire to stop gambling. With headquarters in Los Angeles, each local group is self-governing, self-supporting, nonpolitical, and nonsectarian. It is estimated that nine out of ten who join manage, in time, to shake the gambling habit.

The recovery program of GA involves twelve steps which are basically spiritual in nature.

Twelve Steps of Gamblers Anonymous

1. We admitted we were powerless over gambling —that our lives had become unmanageable.
2. Came to believe that a Power greater than ourselves could restore us to a normal way of thinking and living.
3. Made a decision to turn our will and our lives over to the care of this Power of our own understanding.
4. Made a searching and fearless moral inventory of ourselves.
5. Admitted to ourselves and to another human being the exact nature of our wrongs.
6. Were entirely ready to have these defects of character removed.
7. Humbly asked God (of our understanding) to remove our shortcomings.
8. Made a list of all persons we had harmed and became willing to make amends to them all.
9. Made direct amends to such people wherever possible, except when to do so would injure them or others.
10. Continued to take personal inventory and when we were wrong, promptly admitted it.
11. Sought through prayer and meditation to improve our conscious contact with God as we understood Him, praying only for knowledge of His will for us and the power to carry that out.
12. Having made an effort to practice these principles in all our affairs, we tried to carry this message to other compulsive gamblers.

The serenity prayer was also adopted by GA: "God grant me the serenity to accept the things I cannot change, courage to change the things I can, and wisdom to know the difference."

Recently a member of Gamblers Anonymous lectured in a Christian ethics class at Southern Baptist Theological Seminary in Louisville. After having gambled for twenty years, he was able to overcome his addiction, as he said: "By the grace of God and Gamblers Anonymous." He had lost his home, his friends, his job, his human dignity, and had wrecked his family. He saw his furniture repossessed and witnessed the disassembling of the baby bed which was reclaimed for failure of payments. Today he is a responsible father, businessman, and citizen.

GA has established wives' groups called Gam-Anon. This organization provides assistance to the wives and families of gamblers. Here they can learn to understand the nature of their husbands' problem and how to help them.

Both GA and Gam-Anon welcome with an open heart and helping hand all sincere persons. Experience has shown that together those afflicted with compulsive gambling can recover, if they really want to, and find a life of hope and usefulness in society.

CHURCH RESOURCES

Two factors rise up to frustrate us when we turn to the role of the church in the rehabilitation of the gambler. First, churches have done little in a practical way to help the gambler to overcome his illness. By and large he has been condemned or ignored. Ministers have not known how to deal with the gambler and his problem. Secondly, some churches sponsor gambling in terms of raffles, bingo, and the sale of chances on some item for charitable causes.

Under the guise of religion these churches not only provide incentive but set the seal of public approval on gambling. But in spite of these hindrances, churches must have the courage to care for the welfare of the victims of gambling. They too are made in the image of God and are potential members of his Kingdom.

1. *Theology and Gambling.* A theology that will present a positive answer to the issue of gambling needs to be developed by the church. Such a theology will stress the stewardship of the gifts of God to man.[5]

Christian stewardship includes the totality of one's personality: his time, talents, and property. Leisure time is to be used for God's glory.[6] Gambling is a waste of precious time and is unwholesome recreation. Talents are to be employed in the service of God and neighbor. Gambling is a waste of talents and destructive of one's fellowman. Money symbolizes a man's lifeblood, "coined personality," and is to be used for constructive purposes. Gambling is a misuse of property, for it transfers property from one person to another on the basis of chance without an equivalent received by the loser. Gambling may bring passing pleasure to the winner, but it brings pain to the loser.[7] It also brings suffering to the gambler's family and friends.

2. *Religious Education.* Every church can provide a sustained educational program for young people and adults dealing with critical moral issues. Study groups should be formed to examine the nature, extent, evils, and ways of curbing gambling. Literature, filmstrips, movies, books, and tracts on the subject may be had from the social service commissions of the major religious denominations. Unfortunately many of these materials lack depth and present

negative approaches to the problem. At any rate, lawyers, policemen, social workers, and others in the church and community can be enlisted to provide fresh and first-hand information about the problem of gambling.

3. *Koinonia in the Church.* A former alcoholic confided that when he affiliated with a large city church he could find no intimate fellowship for dialogue and a sharing of his experience with others who were sympathetic. This is a common experience of the gambler who has recovered from his plight through the disciplined fellowship of Gamblers Anonymous. It is imperative that the church create a koinonia, a small fellowship within the ecclesia where people can find more complete acceptance and understanding. In other words, the church must search for ways of ministering to people with problems through its own redemptive fellowship.

4. *Meeting Place for GA.* It may appear as a small gesture, but churches can provide a meeting place and facilities for Gamblers Anonymous groups. Such an expression of concern will let gamblers, and former addicts, know that the church cares about their welfare. It also may be a means of reaching some of these people for Christ and the church.

5. *Pastoral Counseling.* The gambler struggling to overcome his weakness needs personal counseling. A pastor who will render this kind of service without cant or sickly piety can be of real help to his counselee. Frederick West, a clergyman, has written a deeply moving account of the conversion of a one-time notorious underworld figure. Through a series of counseling sessions this minister, using

nontraditional terms, was able to develop a basis of communication with this man who was contemptuous of religion and to win him to the Christian faith.[8]

When asked by a ministerial student how to minister to a compulsive gambler, the GA member made several suggestions. The negative side: (a) Don't tell him to stop, for this will only irritate him. He has heard this many times. (b) Don't sympathize with him. If you do, you have just "adopted a son"! He will use anybody when he is compulsive, even ministers. (c) Don't ridicule him, for this will make him worse. (d) Don't get him to sign a pledge or to swear off gambling—it is a waste of time. (e) Don't give him money, for he will gamble it away. On the positive side: (a) Pray for guidance. (b) Recognize that the gambler himself does not understand himself or how to cope with his problem. (c) Seek to understand the gambler. (d) Refer him to Gamblers Anonymous. (e) If there is no GA chapter in the community, help to establish one.

It goes without saying that the pastor should aim at the gambler's conversion. Even Gamblers Anonymous members know that in order to prevent a relapse it is necessary to experience "certain personality changes within themselves" and that this involves response to "spiritual principles" in order to make them effective.[9] The gambler must be convinced that he has acceptance with God through repentance and faith, and should be led to accept this acceptance even though seemingly unacceptable.

In counseling with the compulsive gambler, the pastor may have to make referral. Hence, he should familiarize himself with all community resources. Teamwork with psychiatrists, doctors, social workers, GA groups, and other sources of help may be necessary in the redemption of the compulsive addict.

What is the pastor to do when he discovers that gambling is spreading in his community and that some of his members have become victims of the gambling fever? Recently a pastor related how shocked he was to find this to be the case in his situation. The first thing he did was to see the city fathers and to call a meeting of the ministerial alliance. When asked if he had counseled with his own church members involved, his answer was in the negative. The minister must have the courage to begin his campaign against an evil force by confronting members of his own flock who are guilty.

This does not mean that interfaith action through various agencies is to be ruled out. To strike an effective blow at a community evil it may be necessary to bring to bear the total religious and moral forces on the issue. Teamwork here is essential. As one Greek Orthodox priest remarked: "We may differ theologically, but we can all fight the devil sociologically."

6. *Committee of Concern.* A committee of social concern composed of capable persons in a church can be appointed to assist the pastor in ministering to gamblers and their families. A Christian lawyer, doctor, psychiatrist, or social worker on such a committee can provide a healing ministry to these desperate and sick persons. Too, this would be a concrete means of involving some church members in Christian ministry who would not serve in any other capacity.

7. *Personal Example.* Gamblers Anonymous points out that the reformed gambler cannot wager the smallest bet without slipping back into the old compulsive habit. Like the alcoholic who with one drink will resume his drinking,

so with the compulsive gambler. He will fall back into the grip of gambling. Hence, the concerned Christian will refrain from all forms of gambling to avoid tempting the former gambler and potential gamblers.

The Christian must avoid putting a stumbling block in the way of a weaker person. Paul admonishes: "We who have strong faith ought to shoulder the burden of the doubts and qualms of others and not just to go our own sweet way. Our actions should mean the good of others—should help them to build up their characters." (Rom. 15:1–2, Phillips.)

Hopefully the above suggestions may contribute to a more comprehensive strategy to help rehabilitate the gambler. Only the surface of the issue has been scratched. Other persons will plow deeper and straighter furrows from which may come methods that will deal more realistically with the problem. As a healing community, the church has a contribution to make toward this end. It must recognize that the gambler, as everyone else, is a person "for whom Christ died." Hence, it must have the courage to care and take the risk involved in ministering to all sinners.

5

HIGHWAY MORALITY

SLAUGHTER ON OUR STREETS and highways by automobile accidents is one of the most serious problems in America. We are killing ourselves at a rate that would shock the most bloodthirsty savages. The problem is so close to us that we cannot see it as an issue of major proportions. There is an element of fatalism in our attitude toward the number of people who are killed and injured on our highways. Indeed, it is taken for granted that a significant number of people will be killed and maimed in auto accidents. In spite of the enormous number of deaths and injuries on our roads, this is complacently accepted by most of us.

This chapter is concerned with some statistics about the number of people killed and hurt on our highways, causes of auto accidents, some positive steps toward prevention, and moral responsibility in driving.

SOME SAD STATISTICS

Statistics reveal some disturbing facts about auto accidents, but few Americans take this sort of research seriously. Neverthless some facts and figures are discussed below with the hope that they might force us to face up to our moral responsibility in the matter of operating motor vehicles.

More Americans are killed and injured in auto accidents in this country than in all the wars we have fought. From 1900 through 1967 motor vehicle deaths totaled 1,650,-000.[1] Deaths of U.S. soldiers in all wars since 1776 total 1,118,000. More people died in traffic accidents in this country in 1969 than American military personnel did in the entire Vietnam war.

Each year new high-water marks are reached in the gruesome toll of death and injury on our nation's streets and highways. In 1912 there were 3,100 fatalities. By 1968 the number had spiraled to 55,500, which represents a 5 percent increase over the previous year.[2] The 1968 figure of 55,500 represents approximately the entire population of cities such as Coral Gables, Florida, and Beverly Hills, California.

More than 50 percent of all highway deaths occur during the weekend from Friday through Sunday with Saturday and early Sunday morning being the most dangerous hours. More than 30 percent of deaths from accidents occur in urban areas and about 70 percent in rural areas and towns under 2,500 population.

A large number of young people are involved in accidents and deaths on the highways and streets. Almost 32 percent of the drivers involved in fatal accidents are under twenty-five years of age. Speeding is one of the major causes of accidents in which youth are involved.

One would think that most fatal traffic accidents would occur during bad weather, but this is not the case. Favorable weather is no safeguard against auto accidents. National Safety Council studies show that the vast majority of fatal accidents occur in clear weather and on dry roads.

CAUSATIVE FACTORS IN AUTO ACCIDENTS

A primary cause of automobile accidents is excessive speed. Almost three out of every ten fatal accidents involve a vehicle being driven too fast. Driving on the wrong side of the road and reckless driving equally cause about 14 percent of deaths in auto accidents. Driving without the right-of-way, driving off the roadway, and passing on the wrong side of the road and on curves and hills also take their toll of lives in lesser numbers.

Almost 80 percent of all accidents are due to errors of judgment on the part of the driver. Indeed, most of the accidents that occur may be chalked up as a tragedy of errors. Failure to signal properly, failure to dim lights, and tailgating, that is, following too closely the car in front, are among the common errors of drivers.

Alcohol and auto accidents are closely related. Studies show that drinking may be a factor in at least one half of all fatal accidents on our streets and highways. "Alcoholocaust" is a term used to describe the problem.[3] A yearlong study conducted in forty-one counties of California show that almost 3 out of 5 of the fatally injured drivers tested had been drinking. In Wisconsin a similar study showed that nearly 2 out of 3 drivers among 369 tested who died in traffic accidents from 1965 to 1966 had been drinking. Almost 3 out of 5 drivers had a blood-alcohol level of 0.10 percent or higher. Similar studies have been made in other states with approximately the same results.[4]

The Highway Safety Act was passed by Congress in

1966. It provided for a federal study, by the Department of Transportation, of the relation between drinking and automobile accidents. The results reveal that about half of the 50,000 annual deaths on our highways are related to drinking. This figure is the same as that stated by the National Safety Council.

Antisocial behavior is closely related to auto accidents. A man tends to drive as he lives. Behind the wheel a man reveals his real personality. In other words, driving is an extension of personality. A driver who has aggressive, selfish characteristics exhibits these traits when he gets into the driver's seat.

SOME PREVENTIVE STEPS

Numerous steps can be taken that can help to prevent death and injury in traffic accidents. Some of them are so simple that they are often overlooked. The suggestions below do not guarantee freedom from accidents, but they will contribute to safer driving. Even the best of drivers can profit by giving serious attention to them. Among the concrete things that can be done to prevent accidents are adequate laws, more programs of education, and defensive driving.

More realistic highway laws are needed. Periodic inspection laws are necessary to make sure that automobiles are safe and to eliminate potential death cars from the highways. Licenses to operate a car should be refused those who have physical and psychological handicaps. A simple driver reexamination test would eliminate many of these dangerous drivers.

Along with more adequate laws there must be enforcement of them. This would mean a better-trained police with up-to-date equipment for detecting violators of the law. More patrolmen are needed, especially on superhighways where so many offenders should be apprehended. Better highway markings such as white lines on the road and speed limit signs are needed.

Uniform traffic laws are needed throughout the nation. Our diverse and chaotic traffic laws are confusing and unjust. Traveling from one state to another, one encounters driving laws that are in direct contradiction to one's own state. For example, in some states a driver who reaches the intersection first has the right-of-way and may turn to the left directly across the path of the oncoming auto. In some states U-turns are permitted and in others one may turn on a red light. Speed limits vary from state to state and some states do not have any laws against slowpoke drivers who impede traffic. These are but a few of the discrepancies in state laws regarding driving.

Also, there is no uniformity in driver licensing. This poses a real danger, for a person licensed in one state may drive in all states. In some states persons may be licensed to drive who are receiving state aid to the blind. There are no laws in Louisiana, Wyoming, Maine, Massachusetts, and New York that prohibit the issuing of licenses to drug addicts and the mentally ill.[5] No uniform standards for driver education exist. Standard driver education programs for young people of licensing age should be required in every state. Indeed every high school should provide courses dealing with driving, highway safety, traffic rules, and the general principles of good driving.

Stricter control of drunken driving is desperately needed. In general it is agreed that it is illegal to drive a car while intoxicated. But there is the problem of what is meant by "intoxication." Some states have passed laws defining intoxication by the blood-alcohol content. Under 0.05 percent alcohol content is a presumption of innocence; over 0.15 percent is a presumption of guilt. But little effort is made to convict anyone unless he has a blood-alcohol content of over 0.15 percent. It is in this gray zone between 0.05 and 0.15 percent alcohol saturation that numerous studies have revealed that fatal accidents occur. For example, a California traffic study of 1961–1965 shows that 76 percent of the male victims of fatal one-car accidents had been drinking and 70 percent had blood-alcohol levels of only 0.15 percent or more. The study also reveals that over 90 percent of drinking drivers killed were at fault and 44 percent of the drivers who were not at fault were killed by drunken drivers.

In Illinois, Delaware, New Hampshire, Montana, and Maryland, studies have shown that there was a sizable number of persons with 0.5 percent (some even less) of alcohol content who were involved in fatal accidents. Obviously, 0.5 percent alcohol content should be legally acceptable evidence of drunken driving.

Furthermore, it is clear that there must be laws that will require testing of suspected intoxicated drivers and laws permitting the arrest of those who are suspected of driving while under the influence of strong drink. A simple unambiguous law could be passed that would make it illegal to operate a motor vehicle with any amount of alcohol content in the blood. Any alcohol content above 0.5 percent could be considered as drunken driving. A lesser fine could be applied to those who have less than 0.5 percent, while stiffer penalties could be meted out to those above this point. While some can drive safely with 0.5 percent or even above, the line must be drawn somewhere and on the basis of statistics and research this point appears to be a fair one.[6] More adequate instruments of detecting drunkenness need to be developed. The "breathalyzer" is now being used in several countries to determine the blood-alcohol content of the driver. Under the Implied Consent Law of Kentucky, the arresting officer will request the motorist to submit to a chemical test. Refusal to submit results in a six-month license suspension. Through special courses, officers are trained in the use of the breathalyzers for determining if the motorist is intoxicated. This technique is now considered to be an effective "tool" in dealing with the drinking driver.[7]

Under the new Road Safety Act in Great Britain, the driver does not have to be drunk to be charged. The offense is driving with more than 80 milligrams of alcohol in 100 milliliters of blood. The fines and penalties range up to $280, four months in jail, or both, along with the loss of one's driver's license for one year.

Drivers suspected of intoxication are first required to take a test at the scene of arrest by blowing though a glass tube into a plastic bag containing yellowish crystal elements. If the driver's breath turns the crystals green, he is given another test at the police station to verify the first test. He then gives a blood and urine sample and a scientist analyzes it and determines guilt. If the driver refuses the test, he is convicted anyway.

This rigorous and thorough method of testing drivers for intoxication in Britain has reduced the population in the pubs. In addition there has been a boom in the taxi and bus business. More wives are driving their husbands home when the drinking places close at night.[8]

Sloganizing against driving while drinking is a popular pastime. Every school boy is familiar with: "If you drink, don't drive." It is doubtful if this and similar slogans are very effective in persuading people not to drive while drinking. Creative programs giving the facts about the dangers of drunken driving via mass media might prove to be effective. As for example, "Operation Save-a-Life" was the name of a program to encourage safe driving over the Labor Day weekend by Station WCAW in Charleston, West Virginia. Two announcers for the station drank specified amounts of liquor between 3:00 and 7:45 P.M. on Friday during a broadcast. Between the drinks, the announcers took driving tests in dual control cars, revealing a slowdown in reaction and extensive loss of depth perception. A panel discussion followed the demonstration, featuring medical experts, local and state police officials, and other law enforcement officials.

The CBS Television Network has presented a series known as *The National Drivers' Test* on a nationwide scale with news correspondents Walter Cronkite and Mike Wallace as narrators. For a full hour the viewer faces every imaginable hazard of the highway, provides his own answers to the questions, and adds up his score. In the 1965 test, the viewer matched his driving skills against approximately 2,000 licensed drivers in the four largest metropolitan areas of the nation. The maximum score was 80. Of the 2,000 drivers in New York, Philadelphia, Chicago, and Los Angeles, the average score was 51. Those who had a high school driver education course averaged only 53, while all others scored about 50. This national test reveals how ignorant the average American driver is about the simple rules of safe driving and the need for driver education.

Federal laws are essential to make the auto safer. In 1965, 20 million automobiles were involved in 14 million accidents. More than 50,000 were killed and 4,400,000 injured. The economic cost was 9 billion dollars. Building safer motor vehicles would cut highway casualties sharply.

But car makers know that styling and not safety sells cars. Hence, they have been reluctant to invest money in new safety features. Members of Congress, however, are pushing for the establishment of minimum safety requirements for autos and President Johnson gave the auto makers until 1970 to comply with federal standards of safety.

In 1965 the General Services Administration in Washington ordered seventeen safety features to be built into 1967 autos purchased by the Federal Government. Fortunately the automotive industry adopted twelve of these safety features as standard equipment on all models. Among these features were a dual braking system and a steering wheel that telescopes on crash impact. Improvements have already been made such as window defoggers, front-seat headrests to prevent whiplash injuries, and padding on the dashboard and the back of the front seats. The crashproof car of the future is in the making and some feel when it comes the casualty rate will be cut in half.[9]

When all is said and done, driving defensively will remain a must. "Defensive driving" is a state of mind in which the driver concentrates on driving in such a manner as to prevent accidents by anticipating the wrong actions of other drivers. The defensive driver avoids tailgating. He keeps a safe distance between himself and the car in front to avoid an accident should the driver suddenly apply his brakes. One car length from the vehicle in front for every ten miles per hour for speeds up to 50 miles per hour is the proper distance. Above 50 miles per hour requires greater distance. When passing parked cars the defensive driver anticipates cars pulling out from the curb and children running from between parked cars. In short, the defensive mentality anticipates all the errors of the less careful driver.

Among the many actions that the individual can perform for safety are: (1) Fasten seat belt or "buckle up for safety." It is estimated that if seat belts were used by all passenger car occupants it would save about 10,000 lives annually.[10] At present only 30 percent of the 90 million cars in the United States have seat belts and only 36 percent of the drivers with seat belts use them all the time. (2) Maintain your car and have periodic check-ups covering the complete vehicle. (3) Avoid driving when tired and sleepy. (4) Never drive while drinking no matter how small an amount. (5) Obey all traffic rules. (6) Keep all doors locked to prevent being thrown from the vehicle in case of crash. (7) Provide your car with all the safety features possible. (8) Carry a first-aid kit and a flashlight. (9) Keep good tires on the wheels. Tired tires can blow out at high speeds and cause loss of control of the auto.

The Golden Rule on the Road

Safe driving on the highways and streets is a religious and moral responsibility. For the Christian it is a sin to drive carelessly and recklessly because it endangers the lives of others as well as his own. The guiding moral principle of driving a motor vehicle is the golden rule: "As you wish that men would do to you, do so to them." (Luke 6:31.) Paraphrased into common parlance, the verse would read as follows: "Drive unto others as you would have them drive unto you." This is certainly the principle that Jesus would follow if he were behind the wheel of a car today. He would have a care and concern for the safety of other drivers as well as pedestrians.

Abbé Hubert Renard shows the relevance of the Sermon

on the Mount for the modern driver. He cites the passage:
"Ye have heard that it hath been said, An eye for an eye,
and a tooth for a tooth." Then he puts it in language all can
understand:

> Ye have heard it said, "sideswipe for sideswipe,
> right-of-way refused for right-of-way refused." But
> I say unto you, "turn the other fender." If someone
> gets in your way at a green light, let him be the first
> at the next light. And whosoever tries to pass thee
> imprudently with a less powerful car, slow down to
> let him do it more easily. I say unto you, love your
> enemies, love those who drive dangerously. They are
> in peril.[11]

Prayer on the part of the driver that he may have a clear
eye and a steady hand could make him more alert. It would
remind him that he is responsible for the lives of others.
One cannot truly pray the Lord's Prayer without including
all of his neighbors. *"Our* Father," "give *us* this day *our*
daily bread," "forgive *us,"* "lead *us,"* "deliver *us"* clearly
shows that the Lord's Prayer is a social prayer which includes the welfare of all others.

The church, as well as the individual Christian, has a
moral responsibility for safety on the road. A church can
provide an educational program for this purpose. Through
the church's religious literature, its members may be informed as to safety rules and their moral duty to abide by
them.

In order to provide a clinical approach to the study of
safe driving, leaders of youth groups in the church should
arrange visits to traffic courts and traffic schools for first-
hand observation. A trip to the emergency room at a hospital could be instructional. Movies, slides, and other valuable materials are available at libraries and safety councils.

Factual data can be secured, much of it free of charge, from the National Safety Council, 425 N. Michigan Avenue, Chicago, Ill. 60611. Also, the major life insurance companies have public information departments that are happy to supply attractive and factual data on highway safety.

A traffic safety Sunday can be observed in the churches.[12] A service of this sort attracted nationwide attention in a Baptist church in Copenhagen, Denmark. The pastor stressed the Christian's responsibility to drive safely, and a signal sounded every eighth minute throughout the service, denoting another death or injury on Danish highways. The worship service was broadcast over the Danish radio and parts were seen on TV. A brief "motorist prayer" was printed with a gummed backing to be stuck on the dashboard of the automobile as a constant reminder to the driver to drive safely.

Some feel that a church should not deal with such mundane matters as safe driving. But a problem more deadly than any disease in this nation is a responsibility of the church as well as the citizen. Human life is a gift from God and anything that destroys or maims it must be the concern of the Christian church. Consequently, highway safety is a relevant subject for every pulpit in the land.

6

POPULATION EXPLOSION

THE WORLD IS IN THE PANGS of "birthquake," an un-precedented population explosion. This is one of the most urgent and important issues facing mankind today. Some thinkers believe that the rapid increase in people is an even greater problem than the control of nuclear war. There is some hope, they think, that the use of nuclear weapons can be prevented, but very little hope that we can escape the astonishing increase in world population. Therefore, all that can be done about the rapid increase in population is to try to stabilize it.[1]

Population explosion may be defined as the present rapid acceleration of the increase in human beings without ade-quate food production available. The fact of the matter is that modern man is eating and breeding himself out of the home right here on earth. It may be that in the long run sexual energy is a greater threat to mankind than nuclear energy. In this chapter we shall consider the nature of this problem, its causes, methods of control, along with some attention to the role of the church in helping to cope with the issue.

THE DEMOGRAPHER'S DATA

Demographers are giving us some startling statistics about the population explosion. At the time Jesus was born, there were only about 250 million inhabitants in the world. By 1650, the world population had gradually increased to the half-billion mark.[2] In 1850, there were one billion people on earth. Producing one billion people took hundreds of thousands of years. Only sixteen hundred and fifty years were required to double the number of the people at the time of Christ's birth. From 1850 to 1924, just seventy-five years, the population rose to two billion, or doubled. Then thirty-five years later, it had increased to a third billion. From 1950 to 1962, just twelve years, the population increased as much as it did from the beginning of man up to 1650. If the birthrate continues at the present pace, there will be four billion people in 1980 and five billion just ten years later in 1990. By A.D. 2000, unless drastic changes take place in the birthrate, the population will be six billion, or twice what it is now.[3]

China with 720 million people is the world's most populous nation. Fifteen million are added each year to its population. India with a population of 470 million adds 11 million each year. The U.S.S.R. has 240 million; the U.S.A., more than 200 million; Indonesia, 102 million; Pakistan, 101 million; Japan, 97 million; Brazil, 80 million; West Germany, 56 million; and the United Kingdom, 54 million.

The United States likewise is experiencing a population explosion. In 1700 there were approximately 275,000 inhabitants in the colonies. The number grew from 1.6 million in 1760 to 31 million in 1860. By 1910 there were 92 million in this nation. From 1910 to 1960 the population rose to 180 million.[4] In 1965 the population was 190 million, an increase of 10 million in five years. Today the population is more than 200 million in this nation.

The United Nations *Demographic Yearbook* (1968) estimates that every day 180,000 babies are born in the world: two every second. The total population rises by 65 million each year, an equivalent of all the people who live in Mexico and Canada combined.

If the present increase in the birthrates in the world continues, disaster may be just ahead of us. The population may outstrip the food supply. If this happens, serious students of the problem predict a time of mass starvation, famine, and war. Already, two thirds of the world goes hungry each day.

The rich Atlantic nations have most of the world's goods. Americans with only 6 percent of the world's population have 40 percent of the world's goods. Most of the hungry people in the world are colored and live in "diet-deficiency" nations. By means of swift and mass communication, they have become aware of the white man's abundance. They have hopes of attaining a similar standard of living as that of the richer nations. If these hopes are frustrated, there may be war between the haves and the have-nots.

One of the disturbing facts is that population is rapidly increasing in poverty areas, particularly in the underdeveloped countries of the world. The population problem, in other words, is highest where the problem of overpopulation is the greatest—in Asia, Africa, Middle East, and Latin America. By the end of the century, if the present birthrate prevails, Africa will double its population, Asia will triple its population, and South America will quadruple its present number of inhabitants.[5]

It is estimated that four fifths of the current increase in people is taking place in low-income societies.[6] Areas with less than 16 percent of the earth's land now sustain about half the world's population. It is in these areas that the population rate is growing most rapidly.[7] In India, for example, where people manage to survive on an average daily diet of seventeen hundred calories (two thirds of the subsistence level) the annual increase is equal to the population of Texas.[8]

CAUSATIVE FACTORS IN THE POPULATION CRISIS

Why does overpopulation occur? Before coming to some specific causes, it may be well to take a look at the Malthusian theory of population. The first comprehensive treatment of population appeared in 1798 when Thomas Malthus, an Anglican priest in England, published his famous work entitled *An Essay on the Principle of Population as It Affects the Future Improvement of Society.* The core of his thesis is that population growth outstrips the means of subsistence, or the food supply. Population, when unchecked, increases in a geometrical ratio; subsistence increases only in an arithmetical ratio. Since the multiplication of people exceeds the addition of food, there will inevitably be more people to feed than there is food.

According to Malthus, the proper balance between population and food supply must be maintained by the decrease in the number of people. In the 1803 edition of his *Essay on the Principle of Population,* Malthus states that "positive" or "natural" checks such as war, famine, and pestilence, along with the "preventive check" or "moral restraint" such as delayed marriage, premarital continence, abstinence within marriage, are means of keeping the balance. Welfare programs and grants to the poor serve only to prevent the natural movement toward an optimum, livable, equilibrium.

Malthus' answer to the population problem has come under severe criticism. Naturally social reformers who believe that the ills of society can be cured and that we have enough technical know-how to provide food for the whole world have rejected Malthus' theory. Students of the problem question whether his basic theory that the population increase inevitably outruns the food supply is valid. Nevertheless his theory called attention to the problem and this was his permanent contribution.

1. *Advancement in Medical Science.* Before the time of Columbus the vast majority of mankind was hungry. This kept the population down due to low physical resistance, pestilence, and disease. Wars were frequent and took heavy tolls on the population. As a result, for centuries man's death rate was so high that it balanced out the number of births.

By the turn of the sixteenth century the population began to increase and today threatens man's existence itself. One of the major reasons for the increase is the achievements of medical science, which has discovered ways of controlling the spread of epidemics and diseases which took the lives of millions of people.

Among primitive people, one half of the children died before growing to adulthood. Until one hundred years ago, one third of all the children of Europe died in infancy. Today less than 10 percent die before reaching the age of thirty. Asia, Africa, and South America have experienced a reduction of infant deaths from 50 percent to less than

10 percent. In these and other geographical areas, longevity has increased twofold.

After World War II, antibiotics and insecticides produced for military purposes were made available to public health programs in many countries. The World Health Organization (WHO) and other agencies have contributed much to the control of tropical diseases such as malaria, yaws, tuberculosis, cholera, smallpox, yellow fever, and typhus, which formerly contributed to a high mortality rate. Hence, the balance of nature has been upset.

A specific example of how the death rate has declined in a particular country can be illustrated by the little country of Ceylon. Due to the adoption of a malaria control program and other health measures, the death rate there dropped from 19.8 in 1946 to 12.3 in 1949. Dr. Robert Hingston, of Western Reserve University Hospital, using a multijet inoculator, stamped out smallpox and yaws in the whole nation of Liberia. Now he has plans to do the same thing for East Africa.

As a result of medical science and improved health measures, a greater number of children reach maturity and have children of their own. So by lowering the death rates and increasing the birthrates, scientists have contributed directly to the exploding population.

2. *Industrial Revolution and Advances in Agricultural Techniques.* The industrial revolution produced enormous increases in the population by the development of machinery to exploit the resources of nature and to manufacture goods on a mass scale. The rise of rapid transportation made it possible to transport goods to communities around the world with great speed.

Mechanized farming has made for greater production of goods, while science has made it possible to breed better livestock and seeds to yield better crops. These developments have made available a greater abundance of food for an ever-increasing population. Even so, the production of food has not kept pace with the increase of people.

COPING WITH THE POPULATION CRISIS

Several plans have been proposed for the reduction of population pressures in various parts of the world. There is even a global strategy emerging for world fertility control. Among these strategies are population redistribution, increased food production, expansion of industry, education, and birth control.

1. *Population Redistribution.* Some have proposed that congested areas ship some of their people to less densely populated places. This has been tried but without much success.[9] At the level of international migration there has been no long-term solution. Since 1821 about forty million people have migrated to the United States. Millions of others have gone to Canada, Australia, and South America from Europe and Asia. Internal migration, the shifting of people from dense to less dense areas within a country, does not solve the problem. For in the country sending forth migrants, there is suddenly more food per capita, which stimulates an increase in birthrate. And the outflow of migrants from other countries increases the population in the new nation.[10]

2. *Increased Production of Food.* It is argued that man now possesses the technical know-how to feed all the peo-

ple of the world. Hence, a step-up in food production is urged. Food, it is claimed, can be had not only from the land but also through new methods of extracting it from the ocean. However, such methods could conceivably present a new and different threat to the previously mentioned balance of nature. Thus there is a call for a radical reorganization and carefully planned use of the economic and technological aspects of agriculture.

Obviously there will have to be an increase in food production in the near future. It is estimated that by 1975 world food supplies will have to be increased by 35 percent merely to sustain the population at its present unsatisfactory dietary level.[11] Suggestions for the increase of food production are irrigation projects; improvement of food-producing seeds and of livestocks; soil conservation; cultivation of jungles; intensive farming; pest control; scientific production of seafoods; and production of synthetic foods. But it is debatable whether such efforts would produce enough food in the immediate future. Besides, where the increase in food is most needed, productivity is most difficult.

3. *Foreign Aid Programs.* Since some nations have an abundance of goods, they could share with the hungry nations through foreign aid programs. This could be done independently by countries or through the United Nations on a worldwide scale.

The United States has made gigantic efforts to feed the hungry of the world through the Marshall Plan begun in 1948, and Public Law 480 (Food for Peace) begun in 1954, which has sent more than $20 billion worth of food abroad. All aid and investment by both public and private agencies since 1950 totals around $70 billion. What about the results? Officials are reluctant to discuss it, but they concede privately that most of the benefits of foreign aid have been wiped out by population increases in those countries receiving aid. Altogether, Western aid during the 1950's helped to increase the income of underdeveloped countries by 3 percent per year, two thirds of which was lost because of 200 million new mouths to feed. That left a net gain of one dollar per person per year.[12]

Now the U.S. farm surplus has been exhausted. At its height our annual food surplus was equivalent to just one cup of rice per week for each of the undernourished persons of the world. And even if we had enough food to feed ourselves and the hungry world, money would be required for transportation of these supplies. There would be political barriers to overcome, as well as the fact that surplus food might wreck the existing economy of the recipient countries.

4. *Education*. To achieve a higher standard of living, education of people is vital. All the fruits of science will be of little value to an illiterate population. In Guatemala, for example, 70 percent of the population over fifteen years of age can neither read nor write. In India 80 percent can neither read nor write. It will take tremendous educational programs to reach the millions of illiterates in these and other countries. How to provide teachers and schools on such a scale is a problem still unsolved. Yet it must be done if these nations are to better their standard of living and curb their birthrates.

5. *Birth Control*. Many students believe that birth control is the only realistic answer to the population problem. Birth control is the voluntary limitation of births by the use

of contraceptives and other devices. There are many of these methods.

a. *Voluntary sterilization.* A simple operation on the male called vasectomy in which the tubes from which the male sperm issues are tied is a most effective means of preventing production of children. This operation does not affect sexual relations adversely and in some cases may increase the sexual drive. The government of India is promoting mobile vasectomy camps and paying forty rupees to men who submit to the operation if they have three children and lack the means for supporting another one.

b. *Legalized abortion.* Another effective way to reduce and to control population is to legitimize abortion. In Japan, for example, where birth control has been a national policy since 1949, there were 20 million legal abortions in the last 15 years or by 1964. During this time the birthrate dropped from 34.3 in 1949 to 16.5 in 1964. About 70 percent of the reduction is attributed to legalized abortion.

Incidentally, the United States is in the throes of an abortion epidemic. One million criminal abortions are performed each year which claim the lives of 500 women.[13] It is already predicted that in the near future there will be available do-it-yourself medications by which it will be a simple matter for women to produce abortions on themselves.

c. *Contraceptives.* The use of contraceptives dates back to ancient times. In the sixteenth century, one Gabriel Fallopius claimed to have invented the condom. Today the condom, the pill, the loop, and the diaphragm, plus numerous other "artificial" means of controlling conception, can be purchased at almost any drugstore in many countries. The contraceptive is one of the most effective means of birth control.

d. *Postponement of marriage and premarriage tests.* The reduction of the population by postponement of marriage is an old idea. Plato, in order to build the good society, advocated the restriction of procreation by law, confining it to men between the ages of thirty and thirty-five and women from twenty to forty years of age. During the American economic depression thousands of marriages were postponed because of a lack of adequate income.

Some today advocate mandatory premarriage tests of age, mentality, health, and economic adequacy which would put restrictions upon prolific baby producers. Later marriages, of course, would reduce the number of fertility years in the marital state. The government could help to lower the birthrate by a tax system which would encourage later marriages and benefit small families rather than large ones.

e. *Public and private agencies.* The Government of the United States has moved cautiously in the direction of providing birth control information and methods at home and abroad. In 1966, Congress passed a bill that authorizes the setting up of birth control clinics in connection with our "Food for Freedom" program. (Our Government is now supporting a number of birth control clinics in this country. Most large cities have such aid at their birth control clinics.)

At present the Peace Corps in two states of India has embarked upon a birth control project. About fifty Peace Corps Volunteers assist officials in publicizing and organizing this program. Worldwide use of Peace Corpsmen in this kind of effort could effectively reduce populations in underdeveloped nations.

Private agencies promoting birth control and planned parenthood are too numerous to list here. There are foundations such as Ford and Rockefeller that spend millions on research in population. Many universities at home and abroad have research centers concerned with demography and family planning. Harvard University has such a project called Ethics and Population in which two professors from the Divinity School participate.

Parenthood Federation sends millions of dollars abroad to groups seeking to spread birth control information to their fellow citizens. Through some 250 clinics run by Planned Parenthood–World Population Affiliates, services are rendered to thousands of burdened families.

THE CHURCH AND THE POPULATION EXPLOSION

All would agree that the population explosion will not be solved by science alone. Human motivation and responsibility are essential for ultimately solving the problem. A viable solution to overpopulation rests with the decision-making of husband and wife. Here is where the church has a role to play. Noah's second flood is rising, but the remedy this time is not to build an ark for a few chosen ones, but to educate the people to see that by practicing planned parenthood they can live adequately in the land which the Lord has given them.

The major churches are concerned about the problem of too many people. They support the *aim* of population control, but differ as to the *means* to be employed.

1. *Roman Catholics and Contraception.* The Roman Catholic Church has largely condemned birth control by "artificial means." From the early church fathers to the

present the prevention of birth has been frowned upon as murder. Augustine even denounced the "rhythm method" involving the calculation of the "safe" period in a woman's monthly cycle because it means having a wife not for pro-creation of children but for the gratification of passion.

The Roman Church bases its objection to birth control by contraceptive means on the concept of natural law. It is claimed that *the* primary end of marriage is procreation. This is its natural purpose. Hence, any interference with the sexual act to prevent the begetting of children is "a sin against nature" (Canon Law 1031, I).

Some Catholics argue that bad results stem from the practice of contraception in terms of personal health, cancer, and sterility. They claim it corrupts the individual since it reduces self-control and emphasizes sex for selfish reasons. But these charges are rejected by some weighty medical authorities and leading psychologists.

It is true that the Catholic Church has begun to modify its position on birth control. In 1951, Pope Pius XII permitted the rhythm method. Surveys show that Roman Catholics are increasingly using preventive methods of contraception. It is also revealed that a number of Catholic doctors disagree with the dogma of the church and recommend the use of contraceptives.

Dr. John Rock, a Roman Catholic gynecologist, formerly of Harvard, helped to develop the first oral contraceptive pill. He declares that it is time to end the birth control fight. He hopes that the Catholic Church will accept the oral pill which prevents reproduction by modifying the time sequence in the female body's function. For example, the rhythm method sanctioned by the church depends precisely on the secretion of progesterone from the ovaries, which action the pills merely duplicate. Therefore, the physiology underlying the spontaneous "safe period" is identical with that initiated by the steroid compound of the pill. Hence the pills serve as adjustments of nature.[14]

Catholic moralists are working on the problem of the pill. They now face the problem of the "retroactive pill" being developed by scientists at Yale. This pill can be taken up to six days after intercourse and still be effective. Two and one half years of experiments have been going on with the use of the pill on rats, monkeys, and people. But the Federal Food and Drug Administration has not yet approved it for general consumption.

Pope Paul's international commission of experts handed him a confidential report on birth control in June, 1966. This commission counseled the pope to modify the church's traditional ban on artificial contraception. But he delayed his decision for further study. In 1968, he arrived at a decision that condemns the use of all means of birth control other than the rhythm method.[15] But many Catholic bishops and priests are rejecting the pope's position and there is the possibility of a radical modification of the church's stand on birth control.

2. *Protestants and Contraception.* Until the end of the nineteenth century, contraception was condemned by both Catholics and Protestants as immoral or unnatural and contrary to divine law.

A change of attitude took place among Protestants from 1920 to 1958 due to: (*a*) fear of overpopulation; (*b*) knowledge of the "safe period" which shows that nature provides her own method of birth control; and (*c*) theological development of the doctrine of marriage. In 1958, the Lambeth Conference did not stress the reproductive end of marriage. Some emphasis was given to love and companionship as ends of marriage.

Biblical revelation, it was agreed, does not limit the function of sexuality to the reproductive activity, but stresses equally the companionate purpose of marriage. Also the members of the conference stressed the responsibility of giving security to children.

In the United States (March, 1933) the Federal Council of Churches approved artificial methods of birth control. Since then several Protestant bodies have adopted the same position. In 1954, the Synod of Augustana Church endorsed it; in 1956, The Methodist Church approved it; and in 1959, The United Presbyterian Church in the U.S.A. adopted it. In December, 1959, the National Council of the Protestant Episcopal Church endorsed birth control. Bishop Stephen F. Bayne, Jr., of the diocese of Olympia, Washington, said:

> Roman Catholic doctrine on birth control, i.e., the continence, either total or during fertile period, as the only moral means of preventing conception, was devised by bachelors on a faulty moral theology which glorifies the single state; it is not particularly observed within the Roman Catholic Church or outside it.[16]

In 1963 a group of Southern Baptists meeting in Fort Worth, Texas, declared that birth control is "both permissible and desirable." Sponsored by the Christian Life Commission of Texas, the stand is not an official one for all Southern Baptists, but it marked the first time that denominational leaders of this faith gathered to discuss birth control as such.

Toward a Theology of Responsible Parenthood

Planned parenthood is a constructive means of coping with the population problem. The birthrate can be lowered by limiting children in terms of one's abilities and economic resources to care for them adequately. Sexual love related to procreation, or begetting children, must be raised out of the realm of biological accident into the realm of decision under God.

1. *Theologizing on Planned Parenthood.* Until recent years, Protestant theologians have given scant attention to the problem of sex and parenthood. Martin Luther and John Calvin, the Reformers, have no specific teaching about the issue. Luther stresses marriage as a remedy for sin, while Calvin emphasizes its communal purpose. Conception, however, in both Luther and Calvin is in the hands of God and interference in his work is sinful.

Emil Brunner holds that God intended coitus to serve as mutual love as well as procreation.[17] This dual purpose of sex is also defended by Reinhold Niebuhr. He accepts procreation as the prime purpose of bisexuality in nature, but challenges the making of this "natural fact" into a universally valid "law of reason," setting bounds for human personality.[18]

Karl Barth thinks that family planning is generally desirable. He discusses the four *means* that may be employed in birth control: abstinence, periodic continence, *coitus interruptus,* and contraception. He contends that they are all "unnatural" in that they involve human interference with "natural" sexual intercourse. Each has its drawbacks: (*a*) total abstinence, the "heroic course," is not wrong in itself, but may be dangerous; (*b*) periodic continence requires discipline on the part of both mates, during the "unsafe period" and even the "safe period" is not safe and causes anxiety by its unreliability and its checks on the spontaneous nature of sexual expressions; (c) *coitus interruptus* is fraught with psychological dangers, its practice may imperil the marital union; (d) contraceptives may be aesthetically uncongenial. Then he adds that if human interference with the natural act of coitus is regarded as wrong in itself, then all methods are wrong including the rhythm method.[19] Barth concludes that the choice made between the various methods of birth control must be made in faith and with a free conscience, and must be the joint decision between husband and wife.[20]

The late Bishop James Pike got into most controversial issues, and birth control was no exception. He declared:

> Responsible choice as to the number and spacing of children is simply one of many areas of life in which people are called upon to make conscientious decisions under God.[21]

Therefore, if a couple ought to have a child, any method of birth control, including abstinence from intercourse, is sinful. But if they should *not* have a child for economic, psychological, or physical reasons, they are under obligation to use the most effective methods to prevent it. "We are not permitted," said Pike, "to use a chance method, like the rhythm method, which some have called 'Vatican roulette,' when a more medically sound approach is available."[22]

Otto Piper, a professor at Princeton Theological Seminary, claims that the "one flesh" passage indicates that marriage is not dependent on procreation because children are not mentioned in the context. Moreover, the passage to "be fruitful and multiply" is not an injunction, but a blessing, a promise of children, not a command to beget them.[23] And Sherwin Bailey notes that coitus is more than a "device" for begetting children. Rather, it is a complex experience involving a relational as well as a conceptual dimension. The relational act of coitus deepens love between husband and wife, relieves their physical and psychological tensions, makes for personal fulfillment, and contributes to the well-being of the whole family.[24]

2. *Principles of Planned Parenthood.* There are no proof texts to support the Christian in practicing planned parenthood. However, there are certain theological principles in the Bible that serve as guidelines for the Christian in this matter. First, the primary purpose of marriage is unitive not procreative. It is the "one flesh" relationship (Gen. 2:24). The primary end of marriage as procreation which dominates church tradition has no Biblical ground. It is based on the passage: "Be fruitful and multiply, and fill the earth." (Gen. 1:28.) But chapter 1 of Genesis is considered as later than chapter 2, which stresses the "one flesh" relationship and the companionate aspects of marriage.

Procreation as the primary purpose of marriage does not appear in the New Testament. Nowhere does Jesus, Paul, or any other writer refer to the so-called command to "be fruitful and multiply," but always to the "one flesh" relationship. Their emphasis is always upon the unitive and relational dimensions of sex and marriage.

Of course, there is no denial of the procreational function in the New Testament and it assumes that marriage issues in progeny. But nowhere does it restrict coition to procreation. Children are assumed to be the fruit of marriage to be brought up in the nurture and discipline of the Lord, but they are never considered as mere biological products. All of this implies Christian freedom and responsibility in family planning.

In the second place, man, made in the image of God, is commissioned in freedom to dominate nature, and human sexuality is a part of creation which he is to control. In other words, man is a steward of his sexuality and must exercise his procreative powers responsibly before God. Procreation is a gift from God and it is the one way in which man participates in the creative process. God does not create irresponsibly but with a purpose. Man imitates God and shares responsibly in the creative process.

Finally, love (*agape*) in the Biblical sense is to will the welfare of others. This applies to the matter of procreation and the rearing of children. Parents, therefore, have the moral obligation of planning for the number of children which they can adequately provide for in terms of care, health, education, and general welfare.

To produce babies up to the limit of biological capacity without the proper resources to support them, or to refuse to have children for selfish reasons is to act irresponsibly. Christian couples, therefore, must, as they understand the will of God, evaluate their own situation, decide the number of offspring they can have, and in the light of love and reason, mutually conclude the number of children they should have and the methods they will use to achieve this goal.

Planned parenthood helps to reduce the problem of too many people. After all, Christians have contributed to the rapid increase in population by social concern and action in combating diseases and saving lives. This has accelerated the birth rate, creating an imbalance between food production and a starving world. Now Christians have the responsibility of helping to reduce the birthrate and feeding those who are hungry physically as well as spiritually.

7

BLACK POWER

"BLACK POWER" IS A SLOGAN of the current Black Revolution in America and symbolizes a new stage in the struggle for racial justice. The phrase gives expression to the deepest longings of the black man who has suffered from powerlessness since arriving in this country in 1619. It is a rallying cry for black unity, dignity, and equality. At the same time it is a threat to the white Establishment and a challenge to our professed democratic way of life.

America's response to the movement which Black Power symbolizes may well determine whether our nation will become a democracy in deed or an apartheid state such as that of South Africa. The National Advisory Commission on Civil Disorders has already warned us that our country is "moving toward two societies, one black, one white—separate and unequal."[1]

This chapter describes the emergence, elements, and radicalization of the Black Power rebellion. Also some suggestions are presented as to the role of the church in meeting the challenge of the racial revolution.

Emergence of Black Power

The slogan "Black Power" was born in the civil rights movement. After James Meredith had been wounded by a shotgun blast in Mississippi, June, 1966, during his Freedom March, leaders of the civil rights movement, Martin Luther King, Jr., Floyd McKissick, Stokely Carmichael, and others, joined the Freedom March. At Greenwood, Mississippi, Carmichael cried: "What we need is Black Power!" It struck a responsive chord in the hearts of millions of black Americans.[2] By July 20, 1967, a National Conference on Black Power was held in Newark, New Jersey.[3] Here the movement was legitimatized in the wake of the Newark riots in which 26 were killed and 1,004 were injured.

Black delegates to this conference numbered more than one thousand. A statement was drawn up that gave definition and direction to the movement. It was entitled "Black Power Manifesto." Two hundred eighty-six black or predominantly black organizations were represented, including the Revolutionary Action Movement (RAM) and the Student Nonviolent Coordinating Committee (SNCC). This was not, as one participant observed, an "integrated" seminar on race relations "to explore the therapeutic rhetoric of brotherly love."[4]

Some of the more significant resolutions adopted by the National Conference on Black Power were *economic*—"buy black," establish credit unions in black neighborhoods, establish a guaranteed income for all people; *political*—establish a Black Power Lobby in Washington, triple the black Congressional representation; *educational*—establish a National Black Education Board, black administrators, and black boards of education in black educational jurisdictions; *international*—develop an international employment service to serve as a skills bank for exchanges by Africans and black Americans and convene an International Black Congress within fifteen months.

Among the miscellaneous resolutions were the initiation of nationwide dialogue on the desirability of dividing the United States into separate and independent nations, one for white and one for black Americans; establishment of a Black Protective Association; and the assignment of only black police captains to black neighborhoods.

This conference may be one of the most significant ever held by blacks. It was a black-organized and black-operated conference. No white liberals had a hand in it. The conference tended to weld the delegates into a unity and to provide an international perspective. It envisioned a worldwide congress of black which doubtless may involve them in cooperative efforts toward the improvement of their lives.

Black Power grew out of the failure of the civil rights movement to change radically the American power structures. By 1964 the civil rights movement had reached its apogee of unity. The various organizations were held together in relative harmony by the tangible goal of legislation for public school desegregation, the integration of public facilities, and equal voting rights. Once these goals became laws, the cohesive factor in the movement was removed.

Enactment of civil rights legislation, however, did not radically improve the Negro's lot in terms of income, employment, housing, education, and social acceptance. Some Negroes felt that constitutional gradualism and nonviolence were ineffective in attaining first-class citizenship.

The hopes and dreams of many blacks for a better way

of life began to fade. The promises of white politicians were not fulfilled. White liberals and moderate Negro leaders moved too slowly in achieving social reform. Negroes became increasingly restive and disillusioned. Consequently, men like Stokely Carmichael, Rap Brown, and Floyd McKissick moved into leadership with the cry of Black Power. Hence, the polarization of the civil rights movement into the moderates such as King, Roy Wilkins, and Whitney Young on the one side and the militants on the other.

Radicals take over when the hopes of the disinherited masses are blasted. The disadvantaged become potentially explosive and may be set off by a rumor or a minor incident such as a routine police arrest of a black person. The poet Langston Hughes expresses it:

> What happens to a dream deferred?
> Does it dry up
> like a raisin in the sun?
> Or fester like a sore—
> And then run?
> Does it stink like rotten meat?
> Or crust and sugar over—
> like a syrupy sweet?
> Maybe it just sags
> like a heavy load
> *Or does it explode?*[5]

Eventually a dream deferred *will* explode as can be seen in the riots, the looting, the burning, and the killing in the ghettos of the cities of America.

Basic Elements of Black Power

Black Power is not a movement in terms of a single organized group. Rather, as Charles Hamilton notes, there are individuals and organizations that fall into roughly four categories: the political bargainer who seeks to work within the system to equalize opportunities; the moral crusader who is more concerned with the "soul of society" than with goods and services, with mass demonstrations and nonviolence than with overthrowing the Establishment; the alienated reformer who stands for local control and substantial changes in the black communities which stress black history; and the alienated revolutionary who feels that little change can be made in the existing power structures and is apt to demand a separate black nation.[6]

Generally, however, Black Power calls for the reconstruction of the civil rights movement around Black Power bases. It challenges Negroes to unite, define their goals, and to place blacks in power to achieve them. It means black political and economic power in their own hands.

More specifically Black Power is made up of a synthesis of radical elements. Some of these may be identified. Black Power means pride in being black. It is an effort to instill pride in black Americans. Stress is placed on the notion that "black is beautiful." It is difficult to convince some whites and Negroes that black is a beautiful color. Even semantics appears to have conspired to make black ugly and degrading. In Roget's *Thesaurus* there are 120 synonyms for "blackness" and about 60 of them are offensive such as "blot," "soot," "grime," "devil," "foul." There are 134 synonyms for "whiteness" and all are favorable, expressed in such words as "purity," "cleanliness," "chastity," and "innocence."[7]

Black Power means the search for self-identity.[8] For centuries the Negro has been told that he is a nobody, an inferior person. Blackness in human beings has become a symbol of inferiority, while whiteness is associated with superiority.

From the beginning of slavery in America, the means by which the Negro could retain his sense of identity were systematically destroyed. His home and family ties were cruelly torn asunder. The Negro image took the shape of a shiftless, immoral, and lazy individual. He was treated as a child and called "boy" all his adult life. The Negro's acceptance of the white man's image of himself engendered a self-hate and a rejection of his color. With the rise of the civil rights movement, the Negro's understanding of himself began to change. In this metamorphosis, the myth of white superiority was exploded. The middle class of blacks enlarged. But the mass of the lower class had been rejected.

The rejection of the lower-class blacks by whites gave rise to Black Power which stresses identification with persons of black origin. Some are attempting to find their roots in Africa. Hence, they adopt African clothes and "natural" hair style. They reject the term "Negro" (a slavery term) and proudly call themselves Black Americans and Afro-Americans.

Black Power means black control and black leadership. Militant Negroes are no longer satisfied with white control of black communities and leadership of black organizations. Carmichael thinks that blacks should own and control their black communities and that white liberals are no longer needed or trusted. White civil rights leaders, he contends, should not organize and lead Negro marches and demonstrations, but rather, organize and lead whites in labor unions, churches, and white communities. Declares Carmichael:

Racism in America is a white problem not a Negro problem, and we are trying to force white people to move into the white community to deal with that problem. We don't need them from Berkeley in SNCC. We don't need white students: "Don't come over where the action is, baby, but start where the action is going to be, i.e., in the white community."[9]

This does not mean, says Carmichael, that he is anti-white, but that black people are too busy with their own work to worry about white people.

Black Power means proportionate political power. It is a demand for majority control in areas where black people are in the majority and a proportional share in key decision-making posts in areas where they are in a minority. For example, Negroes should have 30 percent of the power where they make up 30 percent of the population and 90 percent where the black population is 90 percent. Obviously, this would mean black control of some counties in the South and some cities in the North where the majority of the population is made up of blacks.

Black Power is a call for middle-class Negroes to come home. That is, it is a call for the black haves to make common cause with black have-nots so that all blacks can have what belongs to them. In short, bourgeois blacks, the intellectuals and the middle and the upper classes, must identify with the black masses.[10]

Black Power means black nationalism or a black national state within the United States. It is argued by some black militants that justice cannot be achieved in the white American power structures. Black separatism, it is claimed, would make it possible to build independent political, economic, social, and cultural power bases to be used as instruments of social betterment of blacks.

RADICALIZATION OF BLACK POWER

From December, 1955, the date of the Montgomery, Alabama, bus boycott led by Martin Luther King, Jr., to the present, the black revolution has been characterized by "an ascending spiral of radicalization which has not yet reached its peak."[11] The assassination of King in April, 1968, and the failure of the white Establishment to respond adequately to the Negro's deprivation and alienation gave impetus to the radicalization process.

Lerone Bennett, Jr., senior editor of *Ebony,* describes four stages in the black rebellion.[12] They are as follows: (1) the period of passion led by Booker T. Washington, which was a time marked by suffering and the effort to maintain being without being overcome; (2) the integration stage under the guidance of the NAACP and the National Urban League, in which there was sufficient self-awareness to oppose injustice, but not enough power to force real change; (3) the stage of mass direct action under the leadership of King, a movement that began with non-violent protest, but became increasingly violent when the social structures did not radically change; and (4) the stage of nationalist rebellion led by radical black militants and marked by rioting, burning, and looting.

Hence, the Black Power movement has passed beyond the romantic stage to a more radicalized posture. While Roy Wilkins of the NAACP, Ralph Abernathy of SCLC, and Whitney Young of the National Urban League still espouse the integration ideology and reformism, they are bending more toward a radical stance. Young has announced that in the future the National Urban League might be using confrontation tactics such as the boycott and picketing.[13]

On the ultraleft of the Black Power spectrum are the radical revolutionaries. They hope to transform society through radical changes. They demand a complete overthrow of our capitalistic system to be replaced by a form of socialism. Huey P. Newton, founder-leader of the Black Panther Party, declares that the ultimate goal of the movement is socialism in which the people will be free participants and controllers of the means of production and consumption.[14]

Eldridge Cleaver, a minister of information for the Black Panther Party, also calls for a total transformation of American society in terms of a socialistic society. Much of his time has been spent seeking international support for the Black Revolution.[15]

At this time the Black Revolution is in a transition stage. No one knows what direction it will take in the future. The stress now appears to be on unity among blacks and coalitions with other minority groups in America along with the effort to secure international support in the black man's struggle for equality. Hence, "Che" Guevara, Mao Tsetung, Kwame Nkrumah, and others have become models or heroes of the international black revolution.

Critique of Black Power

Blacks as well as whites have attacked the idea of Black Power. Martin Luther King, Jr., analyzed both the positive and negative aspects of the concept. On the positive side, King declared that it was a cry against disappointment, hurt, and indignities which the Negro has suffered for centuries in this country. Second, Black Power is a call to Negroes to achieve political and economic power to reach their legitimate goals. Third, Black Power is a "psychological call to manhood." For centuries Negroes have been taught that they were nobodies, mere slaves; Black Power is a psychological reaction to this sort of white indoctrination. The tendency to ignore the Negro's contribution to American culture, as seen in many history books, strips him of his personhood. Hence, the Negro must assert his selfhood and achieve a sense of somebodyness.[16]

On the negative side, King thought Black Power to be "a nihilistic philosophy born out of the conviction that the Negro can't win."[17] Revolutions based on hate are bound to fail. When hope is not fulfilled, hate is turned toward those who originally built up that hope. Black Power is both an implicit and an explicit belief in black separatism. But there is no separate road to power and fulfillment. Black Power alone is no more insurance against social injustice than white power. Voting black and "buying black" will not create jobs and provide adequate housing and quality education.

Roy Wilkins, head of the NAACP, charged that Black Power is racism in reverse and can only end in black death.[18] Carl T. Rowan, former ambassador to Finland, declared that Black Power is "a phony cry, a plain old-fashioned hoax," noting that separatism is not feasible and that the Negroes must compete with whites, for there is no angry shortcut to economic security and racial pride.[19] And another black moderate, Samuel DuBois Cook, professor of political science at Atlanta University, Atlanta, Georgia, declared that Black Power is anti-white and that its racist character is expressed in its exclusion of whites from leadership, the call for a take-over of economic and political power, and the general manifestation of frustration and bitterness.[20]

Bayard Rustin, executive director of the A. Philip Randolph Institute and one who helped to organize the March on Washington in 1963, accepts in principle the Black Power movement, but points out seven of its myths which must be transformed into political reality.[21] Black unity is a myth if based upon race consciousness as the sole factor in building a political movement. A generation conflict, lack of a geographical focus, class and philosophical divisions obstruct the achievement of unity on the basis of racial consciousness.

Black capitalism, says Rustin, is a myth, for the black separatist entrepreneur cannot compete with white economic competition. Hence, economic integration is the only viable stance coupled with federal programs to overcome poverty in the ghettos. Reparations as advocated by James Forman is a myth. Forman, in demanding payment of churches and synagogues for their part in the injustice done to blacks in this country, is not seeking to correct social injustice, but to purge the white man's guilt. Besides, his demand for five hundred million dollars ("$15.00 per nigger") or any other amount will have reactionary political effects. What the black man wants is not charity, but a chance at a job with dignity. Furthermore, to attack a nonpolitical institution is to deflect energies from the major political and economic structures.

In a sense, Black Studies in schools is also a myth, for they may distort history and only serve ideological, political, and psychological functions that will further nonscholastic ends. Black Studies may provide college degrees on paper, but not a quality education, for they are provided, says Rustin, by college administrators only for political accommodation.

Again there is the myth of violence which some black militants advocate. Rustin thinks that violence by blacks is suicidal and increases white fear and political reaction. Besides, it is the blacks who suffer from violence as seen in the ghetto riots of recent years. The solution to our ills is not violence, but a Freedom Budget for all Americans which would provide them with a decent standard of living.

There is the myth of separatism which is neither psychologically nor politically sound. Civil rights legislation and the political progress of blacks have been achieved in coalitions between blacks and liberal whites. Throughout the nation, observes Rustin, blacks who are being elected to public office are doing so with the support of whites. The election of blacks in recent years to significant posts in government (examples: Carl Stokes, mayor of Cleveland, and Richard Hatcher, mayor of Gary, Indiana) demonstrate the absurdity of black separatism in gaining political power.

Finally, there is the myth of the Black Revolution. The black struggle for equality is revolutionary, but not in the sense of violent seizure of power. Basically it is cultural in that the Negro is affirming his dignity and demanding a rightful share in the American economic pie. This demand is not revolutionary, but the response to it is, for it means the total reconstruction of society to make possible full employment, the rebuilding of our cities, and adequate educational and medical facilities. Rustin concludes that this sort of revolution will persist until these goals are achieved.

BLACK AND WHITE TOGETHER

If Rustin has accurately defined the Black Revolution, it is a legitimate one. American democracy cannot flower and flourish without all its citizens participating equally and responsibly in the decision-making process. As long as one segment of society does not share fully in the power structures, no one will enjoy the full fruits of a free society. Black and white must move together to achieve the rights of all. Both races must open the doors of opportunity for all American citizens and enter them together to work for full self-realization. The old myth that the Negro should lift himself up by his own bootstraps as did the Irish, Italians, Germans, and other immigrants must be exploded. How can a man lift himself by his own bootstraps when he has no boots? White immigrants who have broken out of ghettos were not hampered by black visibility. Moreover, they were not cursed by being American slaves for four hundred years.

These and other facts the white man must understand. Social progress can only come when black and white work together to remove all traces of any stigma of being black. "We shall overcome" when the "we" becomes a reality and the "you people" approach is buried forever. In the words of the civil rights anthem: "Black and white together; Black and white together today" is the answer. White resistance must give way to white reception of all as first-class citizens of this semidemocratic society. The American dilemma can be resolved only when the ideals of liberty and justice for all become incarnate in persons and power structures.

Why does the Negro who is told that we live in a democracy have to fight for any of his rights already guaranteed by the Constitution?

There are in this nation many "open doors," but there are "many adversaries" (I Cor. 16:9). The advocates of segregation, discrimination, and exploitation of minority groups must be overcome so that all may enter freely through these doors of opportunity.

All must have the right to enter the door of political power. Blacks have just as much right to organize themselves into black political, economic, and social entities as whites do into white power structures as long as these are in harmony with democratic principles. All must have the right to live, work, and serve in open communities. This means fair employment practices, the right to buy and live in a neighborhood where one can afford it, and the right to equal educational opportunities. To implement these basic rights the churches have a strategic role to play. Besides open communities there must be open churches and people in them with open hearts.

In a democracy all individuals and institutions must function together for the abundant life of everyone. White power, black power, red power, and yellow power must contribute to the goal of making and keeping human life human for all citizens. White power alone and black power alone cannot accomplish the good life for all. It takes all the keys on the piano, both black and white, to produce the full music of our national anthem. Only as black and white act together on the basis of equality can we sing in spirit and in truth about the "land of the free and the home of the brave."

8

PROFILE OF PREJUDICE

PREJUDICE IS A COMPLEX PHENOMENON about which the scientists know very little as to causes and consequences. Studies of the problem have not sufficiently explored its basic roots to arrive at any certainty concerning its nature and function. Knowledge about prejudice is like knowledge about cancer at this time. Hence, the modest subject of the "profile" of prejudice has been chosen, for only the main outlines and contours of its ugly face are dealt with. This statement attempts to present the extent of prejudice in the United States, the sociopsychological interpretations of the problem, and a theological analysis of the issue.

THE PREVALENCE OF PREJUDICE

Racial prejudice in America appears to be deep and widespread. Within the past few months the following statements have been made by respectable church members: "I have nothing against Negroes as long as they stay in their place." "As for those who doubt the inferiority of this race (Negro), I suggest that they scan the criminal court records on major crimes." "The Negroes have had their freedom for a hundred years or more and what have they done? . . . They have depended on the white people to keep them up."

In addition to these antipathetic attitudes, we have all been apprised of the brutality of whites against blacks in the South and blacks against whites in the North. All across the nation the intensity of prejudice ranges from mild aversion to hostile acts.

Pollsters have accumulated considerable data on the extent and intensity of prejudice in this nation. In the spring of 1968, CBS commissioned the Opinion Research Corporation of Princeton, New Jersey, to survey current racial attitudes in this country. The study reveals that 43 percent of whites believe that Negroes are not civilized. The survey further indicates that 40 percent of whites think that Negroes have low moral standards; 53 percent think that they tend to be lazy and would rather not work; 57 percent think that they run down the neighborhoods in which they live; 48 percent think that they have a high crime rate; and only 5 percent believe that if given a good job the Negro will make a success of it.[1]

Racial prejudice is discussed almost universally in America as being all on the side of the whites. The fact is that the Negro is also prejudiced against the white man.

Louis Lomax, noted Negro author, declares that most Negro leaders have not been completely honest in saying that attacks upon white people in New York on the streets and in the subways are not racial in character. He says that Negro leaders in NAACP and CORE would have the world believe that gang assaults are nothing more than the run-of-the-mill New York violence carved out by gangs that just happen to be all Negro against the people who just happen to be all white. Some of the killings are clearly racial in origin. Concludes Lomax: "The blunt truth is that Negroes do not, on the whole, love white people; we would be something other than human if we did."[2]

Negroes are brought up like other Americans despite separations and segregation, and therefore, share in, as W.E.B. DuBois says, current American prejudice.[3] But the Negro's prejudice against whites is negative in character, for it stems from fear and resentment of domination and discrimination, not race.

PREJUDICE: SOCIOPSYCHOLOGICAL THEORIES

Social scientists and psychologists usually conceive of prejudice as containing the elements of prejudgment and emotional bias, favorable or unfavorable toward others. Louis Wirth, for example, defines prejudice as "an attitude with an emotional bias."[4] Hortense Powdermaker, on the other hand, says that prejudice means "jumping to a conclusion before considering the facts."[5]

1. *The Sociologist's View of Prejudice.* Sociologists are largely concerned with the external factors causing prejudice. There is universal agreement among them that it is learned in the social context. This dogma is well stated by Oscar Hammerstein in a line from the musical play *South Pacific:* "You've got to be taught to hate and fear." The lyrics of the song expand this theme.

Prejudice, then, is essentially the product of social indoctrination. The individual, declares the sociologist, is not born with prejudice. Rather it is socially acquired.[6] Arnold Rose has very well summed up the social determinants of prejudice as held by sociologists. Among these are personal advantages; ignorance of other groups resulting in stereotypes; racism of the "superior complex"; ignorance of the costs of prejudice; and the transmission of prejudice from parents to children.[7]

In fairness, it must be noted that sociologists do not wholly ignore the fact that the individual does have some natural bent of dislike for others. Egoistic and aggressive tendencies are recognized as native to man, but their direction against particular groups, it is held, is socially determined.[8] It is recognized by some that prejudice may be partly understood as a manifestation of the "needs" of individual personalities that are an amalgam of constitutional and learned forces. For example, prejudice may be an attempt to enhance one's self-esteem or to remove the threat to it.[9] But as a whole, social scientists lay more emphasis upon forces in the social milieu in the development of racial prejudice. All consistently shy away from the older theory that prejudice is inborn.

By way of parentheses, it is interesting to note that communists teach that prejudice is basically a rationale for economic exploitation by the ruling class in a capitalistic society. Hence, eradication of the capitalistic system allegedly would eliminate both race and class prejudices.

2. *The Psychologist's View.* While the psychologist is aware of the external influences that help to determine the attitudes of the individual, he is more concerned to know how these get tied into personality. Gordon Allport, for example, recognizes the sociological factors in prejudice. He emphasizes, however, the psychological dynamics of frustration, aggression, hatred, anxiety, sex, guilt, and projection. While he admits that man has a "propensity for prejudice," he asserts that it is "ultimately a problem of personality formation and development."[10] Personality, he

concludes, is what it is chiefly because of the way persons are socialized (training in family, school, neighborhood).[11]

Most psychologists stress that a contributing factor to the prejudiced person is the ugly stereotype in which all members of a group are judged by the worst of them. For example, three out of four whites in this country believe that Negroes as a race are less ambitious than whites; 71 percent think that they "smell different"; 69 percent say that they have looser morals; 36 percent say that the Negro is of an inherently inferior race.[12]

Stereotyping overlooks the fact that there are superior persons in all ethnic groups. It is the old "lumping fallacy" which lumps all people together as being "all bad." It is a disposition to "over-categorize" and to "think of people in bunches, as though they were bananas."[13]

3. *Reduction of Race Prejudice.* Racial prejudice is the most difficult of all other types to overcome.[14] As someone has observed, the atom was easier to smash than prejudice. Certainly there are no ready-made panaceas for its cure.

Arnold Rose summarizes many of the sociologists' suggestions for diminishing racial prejudice. Among these are awareness that prejudice harms the prejudiced financially and psychologically; accurate knowledge about minority groups; combating racism; legislation; preventing transmission of prejudices by parents to children; direct efforts to solve major social problems, especially economic insecurity; seeking to dispel fears of minority groups; and the development of healthier personalities.[15]

Psychologists recognize the value of all these methods of reducing prejudice, but stress its inward nature and the difficulty of eradicating it from personality. Allport looks at the problem realistically. "A prejudiced attitude," he de-

clares, "is not like a cinder in the eye that can be extracted
without disturbing the integrity of the organism as a whole.
On the contrary, prejudice is often so deeply embedded in
character-structure that it cannot be changed unless the
entire inner economy of life is overhauled. . . . You cannot
expect to change the part without changing the whole. And
it is never easy to remake the whole personality."[16]

In brief, these are some of the suggestions of students of
the problem of prejudice as to its nature, causative factors,
and means of reduction. Accent is placed upon cultural
causation in prejudice, though slight recognition is given
to egoistic and aggressive tendencies in man. Prejudice is a
sociological product. Its cure is seen in education and in
changing the sociocultural patterns.

A Theological Perspective

From the perspective of the Biblical theologian, racial
prejudice is deeper and more universal than is understood
by the psychologist and social scientists. While the theologian recognizes that racial aversion and hostility are
largely acquired in society, he sees its roots in man's sinful
nature. Social scientists consistently shy away from the
notion that prejudice may have its origin in man himself,
particularly in his evil heart. Though sociologist Gunnar
Myrdal does go so far as to say that prejudice is "a problem
of the heart of the American,"[17] he does not mean what
the theologian understands about the heart of man.

1. *Prejudice and the Nature of Man.* Man is a complex
and contradictory being. He is both the glory and scum of
the earth; he is capable of great love and great hatred,
great cruelty and great compassion, unlimited egoism and

incredible altruism. Man's fragmented and contradictory nature is due to his estrangement from God, the ground of his being and existence. Some designate this condition of man as egocentricity, frustration-aggression, natural drives, but the theologian calls it original sin, the sin of pride, self-love, and self-exaltation.

Man is born with built-in equipment for both love and hate. The social scientist's assumption that prejudice is wholly learned "is essentially the smug old doctrine of the essential goodness of man."[18] This presumption that man is inherently good, deriving his prejudice from the social context deals only with the surface of the problem.

Prejudice has a dimension of inwardness which socio-psychological explanations do not touch. Prejudice arises from the depth of personality. At birth a baby is not a mere *tabula rasa* upon which the pen of experience writes and character is determined. Dr. Kyle Haselden has correctly stated that a person "comes equipped with a self which has the capacity for love and a proclivity for hatred."[19] Haselden is one of only a few contemporary writers about prejudice who has had the courage to say that it "is innate, inevitable, yet sinful self-centeredness of the human soul."[20]

Gordon Allport's psychodynamic theory of prejudice may be fruitful to the theologian's attempt to understand prejudice. He notes that the frustration of man's egocentricity and aggressions results in the ventilation of hostility toward some object, and the Negro is a convenient, visible one. Frustration forces him to seek a scapegoat upon which to heap his hostility.[21] But this psychodynamic theory does not come to grips with the genesis of prejudice as a form of sin in terms of man's bent toward self-centeredness.

2. *The New Creation.* Prejudice, we are told, cannot be legislated away, and the sensible thing to do is to recognize it and reduce it as much as possible. But the theologian recognizes the need for a change in human nature, "a change of heart through faith in Jesus Christ." In Christ men become new creations (II Cor. 5:17). In this experience, there is a recentering of personality in the living Christ. This is called conversion. So radical is the transformation of conversion, old things pass away and all things become new.

3. *Healthy Religious Education.* Conversion through commitment to Christ, however, does not mean that one becomes thereby a mature Christian. He must grow in grace and in the knowledge of Jesus Christ (II Peter 3:18). Both his rate and direction of growth will depend upon the quality of religious training received.

Certain types of religious training actually promote prejudice. In his book *Apostles of Discord,* Ralph Lord Roy has shown how some clergymen corrupt the gospel and use it as a weapon of vengeance and hate. Under such leadership a religious mentality is developed that is characterized by racial prejudice and hatred. Persons who do not hold identical religious and political views as the "apostles of discord" become the objects of slander and abuse.

Studies show that religion may promote or reduce prejudice. Gordon Allport and B. W. Kramer, in their study, discovered that "religious training itself does *not* lessen prejudice. But religious training which successfully stresses tolerance and brotherhood *does* tend to lessen prejudice."[22] Hence, when we speak of the relation of religion and prejudice, it is necessary to specify the kind of religion one is dealing with and its expression in personal life.

Christian education should produce healthy racial attitudes. Here our church can play an effective role in the reduction of prejudice. Through their various agencies and media of communication, churches can attack the problem of racial prejudice and mold truly Christian attitudes toward others.

Unfortunately some churches have become captives of their culture, reflecting its racial attitudes. They are often captured and actually used by racists to promote race hatred and segregation. Most of these racists believe they are defending the faith and the church by their actions. Indeed, I have never met a racist who was an atheist.

4. *Confessing to Race Prejudice.* "Confession is good for the soul," and especially when one is guilty of racial prejudice. It will help to ease the conscience and spur one to be more Christian in relation to others. At the ripe old age of ninety, a former pastor in North Carolina wrote an article entitled "I Confess to Race Prejudice," in which he describes his battle against racial antipathy. He was joined in a study of race by a man ninety-five years old, a former professor of Bible in a college. Together they read scientific books dealing with the subject of race. Yet both of these saintly men who felt cramped by custom had to fight hard to be Christian in race relations. Both concluded:

More and more of us are convinced beyond doubt that the whole attitude of superiority is definitely un-Christian and wrong, and harms white as well as black. Our air of superiority irritates and angers peoples of other colors and foments hate and bitterness around the world, and deep within us, hurts our own conscience.[23]

By way of summary, racial prejudice is a multidimensional reality. It is an attitude of antipathy for an individual or a group which may vary in intensity from mild aversion to violence. Social scientists are largely concerned with external causes of prejudice. But the theologian finds its roots in the sin of self-love, and its reduction in redemption through Christ whose glory we behold and through whom we are being "changed into his likeness" (II Cor. 3:18). Therefore the changed individual is to regard no man from "a human point of view" (ch. 5:16). This is easier said than done. But in our struggle to purge ourselves of prejudice, we have the assuring words of Christ, "My grace is sufficient for you" (ch. 12:9).

9

CAPITAL PUNISHMENT

FOR SEVERAL DECADES people in the United States have expressed a growing concern about the validity of capital punishment. Arguments pro and con have been propounded by clergymen, lawyers, penologists, and sociologists, as well as by the general public. In 1960, a Gallup Poll revealed that Americans were about equally divided on this issue. By 1968, public opinion favoring the death penalty had decreased to only 38 percent. But with the assassinations of the Kennedy brothers and Martin Luther King, Jr., the racial riots, the rising crime rate, and the cry for "law and order," there is a trend back toward favoring the death penalty.

THE CASE FOR CAPITAL PUNISHMENT

Advocates of the death penalty for capital crimes often find a sanction for their position in the Old Testament. One of the most popular passages is the one which sets forth the *lex talionis,* the law of an eye for an eye, a tooth for a tooth, and a life for a life (Ex. 21:23–24). Another proof text is found in Gen. 9:6: "Whoever sheds the blood of man, by man shall his blood be shed." But when the exponents of the death penalty turn to the New Testament, they are hard put to find any Biblical support. In Jesus' voluntary death on the cross, some think that by surrendering to its vice, capital punishment was used as an instrument to save the world. Hence, if there had been no capital punishment, there would have been no crucifixion or salvation.[1] Christ is made an advocate of the death penalty by his own statement: "You have heard that it was said to the men of old, 'You shall not kill; and whoever kills shall be liable to judgment [capital punishment].' But I say to you that everyone who is angry with his brother shall be liable to judgment" (Matt. 5:21–22).[2] And Paul's view of the function of the state in terms of not bearing "the sword in vain" is frequently cited as a sanction for capital punishment (Rom. 13:1 ff.).

Beyond Biblical sanctions, advocates of the death penalty set forth several practical arguments.[3] One of these is that the death penalty is a deterrent to crime. It is claimed that the desperate criminal fears the death penalty and to remove it would be to eliminate the greatest psychological deterrent to premeditated murder. A quotation from The Book of Job is invoked as a proof text: "All that a man has he will give for his life" (Job 2:4). The fact that Satan made this statement doesn't seem to matter.

There is the argument of retribution. Since murder is the worst possible crime the extreme penalty should be meted out to murderers as a form of vengeance or retaliation.[4] The criminal who has committed a terrible crime should die. This is even seen by some as the operation of the judgment of God upon the criminal. Again there is the notion that the execution of the criminal provides a symbol around which citizens can rally and renew their strength against crime. In other words, the death penalty serves as a stimulus to encourage law-abiding citizens to work harder in stamping out dangerous criminals.

A more practical argument for the death penalty is that it is a more economical way to dispose of the criminal. To maintain him for life in prison is too expensive. Taxpayers, it is argued, should not have to be responsible for supporting the criminal in prison. "Lifers" will probably spend twenty years behind bars. The cost in prison is about $450 per year. By putting the criminal to death, the state will save about $8,500.[5]

It is claimed that the death penalty provides society with protection against dangerous criminals. This ensures society against the possibility of the criminal's ever returning to commit more crimes. He is to be killed for the protection of others even as a dangerous animal in the community would be.[6] There is the argument that capital punishment protects the policemen and the prison guards. Threat of the death penalty is supposed to deter the criminal from killing officers of the law. This is one of the basic reasons why New York and Rhode Island retain it for murders of law enforcement officers.

In addition to the above statements in support of the death penalty, there is the complaint that abolitionists tend to make no mention of the suffering inflicted upon the unfortunate victim and the grief of his family. Moreover, there is the indictment that crusaders against capital punishment seldom provide any realistic alternative.

The Case Against Capital Punishment

Moral sentiment against capital punishment has been building up in the minds of Americans for two decades.

To support their opposition to the death penalty, abolitionists draw upon both theological and practical sources. They, too, turn to the Bible, the New Testament in particular, to find sanctions for their position. The woman taken in adultery had committed a capital offense under the Mosaic code (John 8:1–11). Jesus not only put her accusers to shame, but also dealt with her redemptively. Jesus would not have been questioned about the execution of the woman which was about to take place had he not impressed the Jews as the sort of person who might disapprove of capital punishment.[7]

Another incident from the Bible that appears to support the abolitionists is seen in Paul's effort to save the life of the escaped slave, Onesimus, who under Roman law was liable to execution. (Philemon.) Paul defended the slave as a brother in Christ rather than entering into a discussion on capital punishment.

But the primary approach of the abolitionists is theological and ethical rather than proof-texting. Stress is placed upon Jesus' teaching of love and forgiveness, even of one's enemies. Love is seen as a redemptive force in life. What hope is there for a dead man's redemption or reformation? Moreover, it is argued that human personality is of supreme value. Man is made in the image of God and no one, not even the state, has a right to destroy it.

Abolitionists answer their opponents who use the Scriptures point by point. It is noted that the *lex talionis* was demanded during the primitive period of the Hebrews and must now be seen in the light of the fuller revelation of Christ. Besides, the Old Testament includes crimes other than murder for which the death penalty is mandatory. To strike one's father or mother (Ex. 21:15), to curse one's father or mother (v. 17), and to be guilty of adultery (Lev.

20:10) all required the death penalty. These facts are conveniently overlooked by the proponents of capital punishment who use the Bible to support their position.

To argue that Jesus advocated capital punishment in Matt. 5:21–22 is based upon a faulty exegesis. Here he is not supporting the death penalty, but simply stating the fact that whoever kills is indeed *liable* to judgment. "Judgment" in this passage means not "capital punishment," but "judgment court" or local village council which dispensed justice. It simply means that one will be liable to judgment before the appropriate court. And the argument that had there been no capital punishment there would have been no crucifixion or salvation overlooks the fact that bribery, betrayal, and mob justice also figured in the crucifixion. Besides, shall we argue to continue capital punishment simply because Jesus was a victim of it?

The contention that the ruler of the state does not "bear the sword in vain" (Rom. 13:4) is not a sanction for the death penalty. The "sword" (*machairon*) is a symbol of authority and not necessarily an instrument of execution by the Roman government for capital crimes. Indeed there is no specific teaching in the New Testament that the state *should* execute a person.

Beyond the Biblical and theological arguments against the death penalty, the abolitionists present some practical ones. For one thing, there is the danger of a miscarriage of justice, resulting in the death of an innocent person. No one knows how many innocent people suffer the death penalty. There have been many cases of last-minute reprieves in which innocent persons escaped execution. Isidore Zimmerman, of New York, for example, was sentenced in 1938 for killing a detective. At the last minute the Governor commuted Zimmerman's sentence, making it possible for him to press his claim of innocence. After twenty-four years he won his freedom when the court of appeals discovered that a prosecution witness had lied and the prosecuter had concealed this fact.[8]

Miscarriages of justice often occur due to mistaken identification, frame-ups, and other causes. Once the innocent person is dead, there is no opportunity for the error to be rectified. Hence, before the death penalty is applied, guilt should be established beyond any shadow of doubt. Better still the elimination of capital punishment would remove the possibility of such a mistake.

Advocates of the death penalty claim that it is a significant factor in deterring capital crimes. Studies prove otherwise. Thorsten Sellin, president of the International Society of Criminology, after exhaustive studies, found no correlation between homicide rates in abolition and retention states. To use one example, in Michigan, which is an abolition state, the homicide rate has remained below that of its neighboring states, Indiana and Ohio, which retain the death penalty. Studies in countries that have dropped the death penalty indicate that there is no relationship between executions and homicide rates.[9] Evidence also shows that there is no relationship between the death penalty and the killing of policemen and prison personnel. A study of police homicides over a period of twenty-five years in eleven states retaining capital punishment and six abolitionist states reveals no significant difference in the states.[10]

Again the death penalty is not applied impartially. It discriminates against the poor and the blacks, because it is more often applied to the indigent, the ignorant, and the unfortunate. A person of wealth is seldom executed. Lewis Lawes, who supervised the execution of 150 men while he was warden of Sing Sing Prison, was impressed by the fact that the majority of them had been too poor to hire a good lawyer.[11] Furthermore, proportionately more Negroes than whites are executed. Marvin E. Wolfgang states: "When crime and color converge, the individual is in double jeopardy."[12] Numerous studies seem to validate this statement. A study of 550 homicide cases in Richmond, Virginia, and part of North Carolina, revealed not a single conviction when whites killed blacks. But when blacks killed whites, over 90 percent were convicted.[13]

Often the death penalty causes undue anxiety to juries made up of those who oppose the death penalty. Hence, it is difficult to get a conviction of first-degree murder. Were life imprisonment imposed instead of the death penalty, there would undoubtedly be more convictions at this level.[14] In 1968, the U.S. Supreme Court ruled that a prospective juror could not be excluded because he had general scruples against capital punishment. This could have the effect of ending the death penalty in the United States.

Finally, the abolitionists note that society must bear some of the responsibility of the criminal since it helps to create the situation in which the criminal commits his crime. Elimination of the breeding spots of crime should be the primary concern of society. Studies show that most murderers who make crime their career come from slum areas where bad housing, poverty, family disorganization, lack of recreational facilities, and inadequate health centers predominate.[15] Hence, the positive approach to crime is the elimination of those factors which breed criminals.

SOME CONCLUSIONS

After examining the pros and cons of capital punishment some basic conclusions are in order. In the decision-making process, the Christian looks not only at empirical data but also to the norms of divine revelation for what ought to be with reference to any moral problem.

First, there is the Biblical view of the value of human personality. Man is made in the image of God and this makes him of great worth. Christ sees worth in a wasted woman, the leper, the child, the man in prison.

Secondly, we are all bound up in a solidarity of sin. Capital punishment may provide a convenient scapegoat for our own sense of guilt. In a letter to this writer, an experienced chaplain of a large penitentiary states:

> I have witnessed some fourteen executions. I have always come away from the execution feeling that one sinner has put another to death. I also come away feeling that this is the easy way out. This is a disregard for the worth of human personality. I feel that this is giving up. I feel that this is a failure to use the disciplines at hand in redemption. There is the discipline of sociology, psychology, psychiatry, and last but not least, New Testament theology. I often come away feeling that our culture is still living in the Old Testament rather than the New. I think perhaps unconsciously that this is the way that acceptable society tries to stamp out the evil that is in themselves. I see that the avenger of the Old Testament has been moved from the family member to a nonpersonal group, the state.

Love (*agape*) is the central ethical motif of the Christian faith. This sort of love is redemptive, always seeking the good of others, even our enemies. How can the criminal be redeemed, however, if he is destroyed by capital punishment? There will be no hope for him to be rehabilitated. Not redemption but punishment is the purpose of imposing the death penalty. This reminds us of the judge who sentenced an eighteen-year-old boy to be hanged until dead in order to teach him a lesson!

On the practical side of the problem, it must be noted that only about 2 percent of those convicted for capital crimes are actually executed. Those who are put to death are not always the most guilty and evil, but the poor, the friendless, and the members of minority groups who do not have the means for adequate counsel. Those who can afford a top criminal lawyer usually receive lighter sentences or even gain their freedom.

Thirteen states (Alaska, Hawaii, Iowa, Maine, Michigan, Minnesota, New York, North Dakota, Oregon, Rhode Island, Vermont, West Virginia, and Wisconsin) have repealed capital punishment or drastically restricted it.[16] In 1968, not a single person was executed in the United States; in the same year, the Supreme Court invalidated the Lindbergh law's provision for capital punishment. And seventy-two countries have abolished the death penalty. These trends would suggest that the value of capital punishment either as a deterrent to major crimes or as a viable approach to the treatment of criminals is being seriously challenged.

In the light of the value of the individual as one made in the image of God, the principle of redemptive love, discrimination in the application of the death penalty, the lack of deterrence of capital punishment, and the danger of executing an innocent person, the death penalty appears to be an anachronism in a society that should be able to deal more creatively and effectively with those convicted of capital crimes. Life imprisonment seems both a more realistic and a more just method of dealing with these persons.

NOTES

CHAPTER 1. MORAL AUTHORITY

1. C. Roy Angell, *Baskets of Silver* (Broadman Press, 1955), pp. 43–44.

2. Karl Heim, *The Church of Christ and the Problems of Today* (London: James Nisbet & Co., Ltd., 1936), p. 99.

3. James S. Stewart, *Man in Christ* (Harper & Brothers, n.d.). Cf. Ch. 4, "Mysticism and Morality," for a thorough treatment of the "in Christ" motif in Pauline theology.

4. *The Oxford Annotated Bible* (Oxford University Press, Inc., 1962), pp. 1412–1413.

5. C. H. Dodd, *Gospel and the Law* (Columbia University Press, 1951), p. 12.

6. T. W. Manson, *The Sayings of Jesus* (London: SCM Press, Ltd., 1937), p. 37.

7. Donald Baillie, *Out of Nazareth* (Charles Scribner's Sons, 1958), pp. 82–83.

8. Paul Ramsey, *Basic Christian Ethics* (Charles Scribner's Sons, 1950), pp. 157 ff.

9. Joseph Fletcher, "The New Look in Christian Ethics," *Harvard Divinity Bulletin,* October, 1959, p. 12.

10. T. E. Jessop, *Law and Love: A Study of the Christian Ethic* (London: The Epworth Press, Publishers, 1949), p. 103.

CHAPTER 2. DRUG ADDICTION

1. Dan Wakefield (ed.), *The Addict* (Fawcett Publications, Inc., 1963), p. 14.

2. John A. O'Donnell and John C. Ball (eds.), *Narcotic Addiction* (Harper & Row, Publishers, Inc., 1966), p. 5.

3. T. L. Duncan, *Understanding and Helping the Narcotic Addict* (Prentice-Hall, Inc., 1965), p. 19.

4. William Braden, *The Private Sea: LSD and the Search for God* (Bantam Books, Inc., 1968), p. 12.

5. *Ibid.*, pp. 14–20.

6. Helen H. Nowlis, *Drugs on the College Campus* (Anchor Books, Doubleday & Company, Inc., 1969), pp. 105–107.

7. John P. Fort, Jr., "Heroin Addiction Among Young Men," in O'Donnell and Ball (eds.), *op. cit.*, p. 79.

8. Department of Health, Education, and Welfare, *Facts Concerning the U.S. Public Service Hospital* (1966), p. 10.

9. *Ibid.*, p. 7.

10. Isidore Chein, "Narcotic Use Among Juveniles," in O'Donnell and Ball (eds.), *op. cit.*, p. 134.

11. James Mills, "The World of Needle Park," in O'Donnell and Ball (eds.), *op. cit.*, pp. 20–23.

12. *Narcotic and Drug Addiction,* National Institute of Mental Health, Monograph No. 2, Public Health Service Publication No. 1021, U.S. Government Printing Office (1965), p. 4.

13. Wakefield (ed.), *op. cit.*, p. 139.

14. Duncan, *op. cit.*, pp. 106–107.

15. See Daniel Casrill, *So Fair a House: The Story of Synanon* (Prentice-Hall, Inc., 1963).

16. *Ibid.*, p. 25.

17. Gertrude Samuels, "Where Junkies Learn to Hang Hard," *The New York Times Magazine,* May 9, 1965, p. 31.

18. David Wilkerson, "Positive Cure for Drug Addiction," *Teen Challenge* (New York, 1963), p. 18.

19. Duncan, *op. cit.*, p. 113.

20. *Ibid.*, p. 114.

21. Norman Eddy, "The Church vs. Heroin," in Wakefield (ed.), *op. cit.*, p. 173.

22. *Ibid.*, p. 175.

CHAPTER 3. ALCOHOLISM

1. Robert Seliger and Victoria Cranford, *Alcoholics Are Sick People*, ed. by Harold S. Goodwin (Alcoholism Publications, 1945), p. 45.

2. E. M. Jellinek, "Alcohol Problems Dissected," *Social Action*, Vol. XI, No. 3 (March, 1955), p. 19.

3. World Health Organization. Expert Committee on Mental Health, Alcoholism Subcommittee, Second Report (WHO Technical Report Series, No. 48 [Geneva], August, 1952).

4. Howard J. Clinebell, Jr., *Understanding and Counseling the Alcoholic* (Abingdon Press, 1956), p. 17.

5. E. M. Jellinek, *The Disease Concept of Alcoholism* (Hillhouse Press, 1960), p. 35.

6. Robert J. Campbell, "The Etiology and Background," in William C. Bier (ed.), *Problems in Addiction: Alcohol and Drug Addiction* (Fordham University Press, 1962), p. 64.

7. Edith S. Lisansky, "Clinical Research and Psychological Tests," in Ruth Fox (ed.), *Alcoholism: Behavioral Research, Therapeutic Approaches* (Springer Publishing Company, Inc., 1967), p. 4.

8. Neil Kessel and Henry Walton, *Alcoholism* (Penguin Books, Inc., 1965), pp. 56–68.

9. Karl A. Menninger, *Man Against Himself* (Harcourt, Brace & Company, Inc., 1938), p. 169.

10. Lawrence Wooley, in Foreword to Seliger and Cranford, *op. cit.*, p. x.

11. Clinebell, *op. cit.*, p. 41.

12. Ruth Fox, in *Treatment of Chronic Alcoholism* (The Medical Clinics of North America. W. B. Saunders Company, May, 1958), p. 813.

13. Ronald J. Catanzaro, "Psychiatric Aspects of Alcoholism," in David J. Pittman (ed.), *Alcoholism* (Harper & Row, Publishers, Inc., 1967), p. 38; cf. a similar list by Percy M. Sessions, "Social Casework Treatment with the Focus on the Image of Self," in Ruth Fox (ed.), *op. cit.*, pp. 302–304.

14. Clinebell, *op. cit.*, p. 233.

15. Ruth Fox (ed.), *op. cit.*, pp. 44–45.

16. Kessell and Walton, *op. cit.*, p. 73.

17. *Ibid.*

18. *The Works of Plato,* "The Laws," Vol. 4, Book II, tr. by Benjamin Jowett (The Dial Press, Inc., n.d.), pp. 405–407.

19. See Jellinek, *op. cit.,* Appendix A, which contains paragraphs from a paper by J. E. Todd on "Drunkenness a Vice, Not a Disease."

20. Clinebell, *op. cit.,* pp. 157–162.

21. Jellinek, *op. cit.,* Ch. III.

22. Seliger and Cranford, *op. cit.,* p. 2.

23. Carroll Wise, *Religion in Illness and Health* (Harper & *Brothers,* 1942), p. 37.

24. John C. Ford, S.J., in Bier (ed.), *op. cit.,* pp. 42–43.

25. *Ibid.,* p. 43.

26. See Everett Tilson, *Should Christians Drink?* (Abingdon Press, 1957), pp. 15–36.

27. Roland Bainton, "Total Abstinence and Biblical Principles," *Christianity Today,* July 7, 1958, p. 6.

28. Harry M. Tiebout, "Conversion as a Psychological Phenomenon (in the Treatment of the Alcoholic)," *Pastoral Psychology,* Vol. II, No. 13 (April, 1951), p. 28.

29. Francis W. McPeek, in *Alcohol, Science and Society* (Quarterly Journal of Studies on Alcohol, 1946), p. 417.

30. Menninger, *op. cit.,* p. 182.

31. Clinebell, *op. cit.,* p. 17; see also *Alcoholics Anonymous Comes of Age* (Harper & Brothers, 1957), p. 68.

32. "The Act of Surrender in the Therapeutic Process with Special Reference to Alcoholism," *Quarterly Journal of Studies on Alcohol,* Vol. X (1949), p. 50.

33. Clinebell, *op. cit.,* pp. 176–177.

34. E. A. Verdery, "The Clergy and Alcoholism," in Ruth Fox (ed.) *op. cit.,* p. 282.

35. Clinebell, *op. cit.,* pp. 179–182; for clinically tested principles of counseling alcoholics, see Verdery, *loc. cit.,* pp. 283–284.

36. Milton Maxwell, "Alcoholics Anonymous: An Interpretation," in Pitman (ed.), *op. cit.,* p. 211.

37. *Alcoholics Anonymous* (Works Publishing Co., 1950), pp. 71–72.

38. Clinebell, *op. cit.,* pp. 143–144, notes that this AA prayer has been traced to Reinhold Niebuhr who says: "Of

course it may have been spooking around for years, even centuries, but I don't think so. I honestly believe that I wrote it myself." See *The AA Grapevine,* January, 1950, p. 6.

39. For more information, call your local Alcoholics Anonymous group or write to the General Service Board of Alcoholics Anonymous, Box 459, Grand Central Annex, New York, N.Y. 10017.

CHAPTER 4. GAMBLING

1. Iago Galdson, "The Psychodynamics of the Triad: Alcoholism, Gambling, and Superstition," *Mental Hygiene,* Vol. XXXV (1951), pp. 589–598.

2. "Dostoevsky and Parricide," *The Complete Psychological Works of Sigmund Freud,* Vol. XXI, ed. by James Strachey (London: Hogarth Press, Ltd., 1961), pp. 193–194.

3. Ralph R. Greenson, "On Gambling," *American Image,* Vol. IV (1947), pp. 61–77.

4. *Gamblers Anonymous-Big Book* and pamphlets may be obtained from the National Service Office, Gamblers Anonymous, Los Angeles, Calif. 90006.

5. See Lycurgus Starkey, Jr., *Money, Mania, and Morals: The Churches and Gambling* (Abingdon Press, 1964), pp. 114–119, for a step in the right direction toward theology and gambling.

6. See Robert Lee, *Religion and Leisure in America* (Abingdon Press, 1964), Part Four.

7. W. D. Mackenzie, *The Ethics of Gambling* (Chicago Theological Seminary Press, 1877), p. 9.

8. Frederick West, *God's Gambler* (Prentice-Hall, Inc., 1964).

9. *Gamblers Anonymous, Questions and Answers About the Problem of Compulsive Gambling and the G.A. Recovery Program* (G.A. Publishing Co., rev. ed., March, 1967), pp. 2–3.

CHAPTER 5. HIGHWAY MORALITY

1. *Accident Facts* (National Safety Council, 1968), p. 63.

2. *Accident Facts,* Preliminary Condensed Edition (National Safety Council, 1969), p. 2.

3. *Alcoholocaust* (Hartford, Conn.: The Travelers Insurance Companies, 1969).

4. *Accident Facts* (National Safety Council, 1967), p. 52.

5. Abraham Ribicoff, "Harmony on the Highways," *The Atlantic Monthly,* July, 1965, p. 81.

6. William Plymat, "We Need an Intermediate Offensive on the Drinking Driver," *Congressional Record,* Aug. 11, 1958, p. 1.

7. *News,* Department of Public Information News Division, Commonwealth of Kentucky, Oct. 15, 1968, pp. 29–30.

8. *The New York Times,* Oct. 22, 1967, 2B, Sec. 4.

9. "Why Cars Must—and Can—Be Made Safer," *Time,* April 1, 1966, pp. 26–27.

10. *Accident Facts* (National Safety Council, 1968), p. 53.

11. Abbé Hubert Renard, *The Automobilist and Christian Morality,* cited in *Time,* May 3, 1968, p. 62.

12. See *Church and Safety,* published by the National Safety Council, 425 N. Michigan Avenue, Chicago, Ill. 60611.

CHAPTER 6. POPULATION EXPLOSION

1. John D. Rockefeller, III, "Population: Decision by Default," *Population Bulletin* (Washington, D.C.: Population Reference Bureau, Inc.), July, 1963, p. 86.

2. Karl Sax, *The Population Explosion* (Foreign Policy Association, Inc.), Headline Series No. 120, Nov. 20, 1956, p. 10.

3. Arthur McCormack, "Food and People," *Commonweal,* Vol. LXX (April 10, 1964), p. 79.

4. Frederich Osborn, *This Crowded World* (Public Affairs Pamphlets, 1960), p. 8.

5. McCormack, *loc. cit.,* p. 79.

6. R. M. Flagley, "Population Explosion Today," *The Christian Century,* Vol. LXXIX (June 6, 1962), p. 711.

7. Stephen F. Bayne, Jr., "Responsible Parenthood and the Population Problem," *Ecumenical Review,* Vol. XIII (October, 1960), p. 25.

8. J. A. O'Brien, "Population Explosion Demands World-wide Action," *The Christian Century,* Vol. LXXI (Jan. 8, 1964), p. 43.

9. L. Burch and Elmer Pendell, *Human Breeding and Survival* (Penguin Books, Inc., 1947), p. 97.

10. *Ibid.,* pp. 87–88.

11. McCormack, *loc. cit.,* p. 80.

12. *Newsweek,* July 23, 1961, p. 30.

13. *Newsweek,* Nov. 14, 1966.

14. John Rock, *The Time Has Come: A Catholic Doctor's Proposals to End the Battle Over Birth Control* (Alfred A. Knopf, Inc., 1963).

15. "Humanae Vitae," Encyclical Letter of His Holiness Paul VI, in *The Pope Speaks, The Church Documents Quarterly,* Vol. 13, No. 4 (Winter, 1969), pp. 329–346; see also *On the Regulation of Birth,* Encyclical Letter of His Holiness Paul VI (Rome: Vatican Polyglot Press, 1968).

16. Stephen F. Bayne, Jr., quoted in *Time,* Dec. 21, 1959, p. 58.

17. Emil Brunner, *The Divine Imperative* (The Westminster Press, 1947), p. 367.

18. Reinhold Niebuhr, *The Nature and Destiny of Man* (Charles Scribner's Sons, 1951), pp. 171–172, 228–232, 235–240, 281–282.

19. Karl Barth, *Church Dogmatics,* Vol. III (Edinburgh: T. & T. Clark, 1961), pp. 269–285.

20. *Ibid.*

21. James Pike, quoted in *Time,* Dec. 21, 1959, p. 58.

22. *Ibid.*

23. Otto Piper, *The Christian Interpretation of Sex* (Charles Scribner's Sons, 1951), p. 51.

24. Sherwin Bailey, *The Mystery of Love and Marriage* (Harper & Brothers, 1950), Ch. VIII.

CHAPTER 7. BLACK POWER

1. *Report of the National Advisory Commission on Civil Disorders* (Bantam Books, Inc., 1968), p. 1.

2. For details, see Martin Luther King, Jr., *Where Do We*

Go from Here: Chaos or Community? (Harper & Row, Publishers, Inc., 1967), pp. 23–29.

3. Chuck Stone, "The National Conference on Black Power," in F. B. Barbour (ed.), *The Black Power Revolt* (Extending Horizons Books, 1968), p. 189.

4. *Ibid.*, p. 191.

5. Langston Hughes, "Dream Deferred," *The Panther and the Lash* (Alfred A. Knopf, Inc., 1967).

6. Charles V. Hamilton, "An Advocate of Black Power Defines It," in Robert Scott and Wayne Brockriede, *The Rhetoric of Black Power* (Harper & Row, Publishers, Inc., 1969), pp. 178–179.

7. King, *op. cit.*, p. 41.

8. Phillip Huckaby, "The Black Identity Crisis," *Theology Today,* Vol. XXIV, No. 4 (January, 1968), pp. 498–506.

9. Lerone Bennett, Jr., "Stokely Carmichael: Architect of Black Power," *Ebony,* September, 1966, p. 30.

10. *Ibid.*

11. Lerone Bennett, Jr., "Of Time, Space, and Revolution," *Ebony,* Special Edition, August, 1969, p. 32.

12. *Ibid.*, pp. 32–33.

13. See Whitney Young, *Beyond Racism* (McGraw-Hill Book Company, Inc., 1969), for Young's basic position.

14. Huey Newton, "The Black Panther Party," *Ebony,* August, 1969, pp. 106–112.

15. See Eldridge Cleaver, *Soul on Ice* (Dell Publishing Co., Inc., 1968).

16. King, *op. cit.*, pp. 32–43.

17. *Ibid.*, p. 44.

18. Roy Wilkins, *The Crisis,* Vol. 73, No. 7 (Aug.–Sept., 1966), p. 354.

19. Carl T. Rowan, "Crisis in Civil Rights Leadership," *Ebony,* November, 1966, pp. 27–38.

20. Samuel Cook, "The Tragic Myth of Black Power," *The New South,* Vol. 21, No. 3 (Summer, 1966), pp. 58–64.

21. Bayard Rustin, "The Myths of the Black Revolt," *Ebony,* August, 1969, pp. 96–104.

Chapter 8. Profile of Prejudice

1. *White and Negro Attitudes Towards Race Related Issues and Activities* (Opinion Research Corporation of Princeton, New Jersey, July 9, 1968), pp. 2–3.

2. Louis Lomax, "From Negro to Negroes: 'Cool Off Awhile,'" *Courier-Journal,* July 5, 1964, Sec. 4.

3. W. E. B. DuBois, *Dusk of Dawn* (Harcourt, Brace & Company, Inc., 1940), p. 191.

4. Louis Wirth, "Race and Public Policy," *The Scientific Monthly,* Vol. 58 (1944), p. 303.

5. Hortense Powdermaker, *Probing Our Prejudices* (Harper & Brothers, 1941), p. 1.

6. Robert MacIver and Charles Page, *Society* (Rinehart & Company, 1950), p. 407.

7. Arnold Rose, *The Roots of Prejudice* (Paris: UNESCO, 1951).

8. MacIver and Page, *op. cit.,* p. 407.

9. George Simpson and J. Milton Yinger, *Racial and Cultural Minorities* (Harper & Brothers, 1953), pp. 66, 83.

10. Gordon Allport, *The Nature of Prejudice* (Doubleday & Company, Inc., 1958), p. 39.

11. *Ibid.,* p. 203.

12. *Newsweek,* Oct. 21, 1963, p. 50.

13. Quoted by Bruce Berry, *Race and Ethnic Relations,* 2d ed. (Houghton Mifflin Company, 1958), p. 371.

14. See Reinhold Niebuhr, "Intractability of Race Prejudice," *Christianity and Crisis,* Vol. 22 (Oct. 29, 1962), p. 181.

15. Rose, *op. cit.,* pp. 37–40.

16. Allport, *op. cit.,* pp. 466–467.

17. Gunnar Myrdal, *The American Dilemma,* rev. ed. (Harper & Row, Publishers, Inc., 1962), p. xlvii.

18. J. C. Furnas, *Goodbye to Uncle Tom* (William Sloan Associates, Inc., 1956), p. 317.

19. Kyle Haselden, *The Racial Problem in Christian Perspective* (Harper & Brothers, 1959), p. 78.

20. *Ibid.,* p. 76.

21. Allport, *op. cit.,* p. 333.

22. Gordon Allport and B. W. Kramer, "Some Roots of Prejudice," *Journal of Psychology,* Vol. 22 (1946), p. 38.

23. S. L. Morgan, Sr., "I Confess to Race Prejudice," *Western Recorder,* March 15, 1962, p. 7. This is a weekly publication of the Kentucky Baptist Convention.

Chapter 9. capital punishment

1. J. J. Vellenga, "Is Capital Punishment Wrong?" *Christianity Today,* Oct. 12, 1959, p. 9.

2. *Ibid.,* p. 12.

3. See Robert G. Caldwell, "Why Is the Death Penalty Retained?" in Thorsten Sellin (ed.), *The Annals of the American Academy of Political and Social Science,* Vol. 284 (November, 1952), pp. 45–63.

4. Lewis E. Lawes, "Capital Punishment," *Encyclopedia Americana,* 1963 ed., Vol. 5, p. 562.

5. *Ibid.,* pp. 562–563.

6. See Jacques Barzun, "Mr. Barzun and Capital Punishment," *The American Scholar,* Vol. 31, No. 2 (Spring, 1962), p. 182.

7. Charles Milligan, "Capital Punishment: A Christian Approach," *Social Action,* Vol. 27, No. 8 (April, 1961), p. 18.

8. Franklin H. Williams, "Double Jeopardy: Black and Poor," *Vital Speeches of the Day,* Vol. XXXV, No. 9 (Feb. 15, 1969), p. 273.

9. *Ibid.,* p. 274; see also Sellin (ed.), *loc. cit.*

10. *Ibid.*

11. Lawes, *loc. cit.,* p. 563.

12. Marvin E. Wolfgang, cited by Williams, *loc. cit.,* p. 275.

13. Williams, *loc. cit.,* p. 276.

14. Lawes, *loc. cit.,* p. 563.

15. *Ibid.*

16. Capital punishment may be applied in New York for killing a peace officer on duty and to convicts under life sentence who commit murder in prison or try to escape; in Rhode Island the death penalty may be applied for murder while under life sentence, and in Vermont for an unrelated second first-degree murder and for killing an officer or prison personnel.